A handbook for teaching in the ghetto school

A handbook for teaching in the ghetto school

SIDNEY TRUBOWITZ

Chicago | *Quadrangle Books*

Preface

Most people agree that the quality of education in depressed-area schools stands in dire need of improvement. Professional educators indicate the critical importance of preparing more and better-qualified teachers for these schools. Civil rights groups almost daily decry what they describe as inferior education in ghetto schools. Boards of education seek every device to persuade more experienced teachers to transfer to schools in the ghetto. And the low results of standardized student tests add further evidence to the argument.

A major reason for the inadequate supply of qualified teachers is the reluctance of many teaching graduates to accept positions in depressed-area schools. It may be a result of the image they have of these schools through sensational news reports and films. Possibly they fear violence or physical attack, or foresee

5

a classroom situation in which all semblance of control disappears. They may think they will be unable to teach what seems to be an unrealistic curriculum. They may feel unprepared to deal with values of language, personal hygiene, and manners quite different from their own.

Those teachers who do accept positions in ghetto schools are often ill equipped to deal with the situations they meet. So some flee the area seeking positions elsewhere, and others develop rigid teaching patterns which enable them to maintain their sense of equilibrium but which do not make for optimum learning for the children.

The educational principles which are part of a thorough teacher preparation program are particularly important for the teacher of low socioeconomic area children. But even more is needed to teach underprivileged children successfully. The teacher of slum children needs to understand the values of his students. He needs to examine his own responses to those values. He needs to know about curriculum approaches that make contact with the children, about instructional materials that have within them the sense of reality that can make for pupil growth. He needs ideas about how to set up relationships with the children that will create an atmosphere most conducive to learning. He must be prepared to deal effectively with deviations from normal behavior. He needs a deep knowledge of the community from which underprivileged children come, of the parents, and of the pupils themselves, so that this knowledge can be applied to the educational environment. He needs especially sensitive supervision, so that he can get support in times of stress and be guided toward the self-knowledge that is so essential for the teacher of ghetto children.

No written material can replace the professional growth that comes with prolonged contact with a school, its children, and a community. But the information in this book may increase a teacher's familiarity with ghetto elementary schools; it may suggest experiences that will better prepare the prospective teacher for teaching in these schools; and it may give him ideas he can use.

This book illustrates how teachers can develop meaningful curriculum content by knowing children's experiences, their interests, their feelings, their needs, their strengths, and their weaknesses. It attempts to help teachers understand a school and a community in the ghetto by exposing them to the perceptions of the children, the parents, and other people in the neighborhood. It shows how teacher awareness of the children's world can help to give depressed-area children a greater mastery of the world and aid them in extending their view of their surroundings. It indicates materials which can be put to effective use in working with children. And it describes typical causes of difficulty for new teachers and seeks to provide insights into problems which may be encountered.

The material upon which this book is based was gathered through interviews with teachers who have achieved unusual success in elementary schools in Harlem; through group interviews with children attending a Harlem elementary school; through talks with representatives of community agencies intimately involved with the school; and through questionnaire responses of supervisors working in the Harlem area. The ideas presented here were elaborated and substantiated by a close, detailed study of the efforts of one teacher to achieve success in a Harlem elementary school; by an investigation of a Harlem community; and by an examination of literature pertinent to beginning teaching in the ghetto.

This book does not try to describe general teaching methods for all areas of the curriculum; that kind of information is readily available in professional literature. Rather, it attempts to deal with teaching methods that apply especially to children in ghetto neighborhoods.

The major focus of the book is to help new and prospective

7

teachers in ghetto elementary schools. But it may also have value for experienced teachers in that it offers the working ideas of skillful colleagues, opens up possible areas of further investigation, and presents a broader view of what it means to teach in a low socioeconomic area.

Acknowledgments

My sincere thanks are due to many people whose cooperation, assistance, and guidance made this book possible. In particular:

The pupils, teachers, and supervisors of P.S. 79, Manhattan, without whose time, thoughts, and interest the material for the book could not have been collected.

The representatives of the Harlem community, who contributed their ideas.

The supervisors and teachers of P.S. 184, Manhattan, for their contribution to the collection of information.

Staff members of the Education and Publications department of the Anti-Defamation League of B'nai B'rith for their advice, consultation, and editorial suggestions.

Dr. Marvin Taylor of Queens College, for his helpful suggestions.

9

Acknowledgments

Dr. Alice Miel of Teachers College, Columbia University, for her encouragement and her many pertinent suggestions.

My wife, Naomi, for her help in editing the manuscript, her suggestions regarding content and form, and, most of all, her listening ear and heart.

Contents

Preface 5
Acknowledgments 9
1 What is the world I enter? 15
2 How can I make it with the kids? 22
3 How do they do it? 41
4 What do the children have to say? 59
5 What can I teach? 71
6 What materials can help? 115
7 What is the community like? 127
8 What challenges remain? 141
Appendix A. Books for children 147
Appendix B. Books for teachers 156
Bibliography 163
Index 169

A handbook for teaching in the ghetto school

1 What is the world I enter?

The teacher in the ghetto elementary school, like all teachers in all classrooms, is faced with diverse problems. In East Harlem elementary schools the difficulty is magnified by the fact that the feelings, experiences, backgrounds, values, strengths, and deficiencies of the children may be far removed from the teacher's past and foreign to his present perception of human existence.

A teacher can always remain like the teacher who said, "It was as if I were trying to reach the children through a pane of glass. They seemed so remote and uninterested."

Or the teacher can become like the one who said, "Teaching here is like taking a Rorschach and getting it interpreted. Pretty quickly you come to grips with your attitudes and feelings regarding such things as cursing, fighting, and cleanliness. When you begin to know what's in your own mind about these and other things, then you can begin to understand what's in the minds of the kids."

A successful teacher in a ghetto elementary school uses teaching procedures that demand a kind of dual vision. He looks at the children and the community and at the same time examines his own reactions to what he sees.

THE CHALLENGE

Listen as a third-grade child poses a question for his teacher. "Do you know why the Empire State Building was built downtown?" The child replies to his own question, "Because the sky is too low up here."

Watch a child on a trip with his class to the Metropolitan Museum of Art as he pauses for a moment at the magnificent area surrounding the fountain. He says, "This is only for white people, isn't it? It's too beautiful for colored people."

Study the following remarks of children responding to a question about what they would like to see changed in their neighborhood:

"I would like to see the streets cleaner."

"I would like to see the building superintendents dressed better."

"I would like better homes and projects."

"I would like to be able to go into my building without being afraid of people."

Hear the children as they talk about the "good life" they so fervently desire.

Walk slowly up and down a street in the ghetto. Allow the life there to seep into your being. Fight past the rigid perception that comes of the fear of strangeness and see the forces that whirl around the children who will sit in your class the day you become a teacher in the elementary school in the area. On

16

certain days you may see a policeman place a shabby man with his hands against the wall and frisk him. Children may walk by only mildly interested. You may see a sanitation worker hurl a garbage can cover at a rat that scurries past. You will likely see groups of men aimlessly drinking beer from cans hidden by brown paper bags. Children will probably be playing with tin cans or sticks in a rubble-filled lot, apart from the dull meanderings of nearby adults.

Go through the outdoor markets in the neighborhood. Feel the vitality of the people swirling around stores and stalls. Watch the children as they run to greet a teacher from their school. Breathe in the odors of the weekly Saturday pork chop fry held in front of a storefront church, and absorb the gaiety. Dwell on the pride-filled faces of adults as a class of children takes a neighborhood walk. Note the watchful care of a ten-year-old child as he leads a younger brother or sister to school. View the uncomplicated joy of the child whose teacher has taken a moment to joke with him.

Follow a child into his home. Walk into halls lit by one weak bulb. See his home with double-decked beds, with a television set blaring day and night, with half-dressed children hanging weakly to a skirt as you, the stranger, enter.

Look at the scrubbed faces, the starched dresses, the suit jackets of kindergarten children as they venture forth for their first day at school. Watch as sixth-graders enter the building for their last day of elementary school, the girls wearing dresses white from careful laundering, the boys clad in suits neat from pressing.

Note the words of the parent who advises the teacher to let her know if her child is misbehaving, promising that she will beat the offender in front of the class.

Read the literature of the civil rights groups that emphasizes the inferiority of ghetto schools and their teachers.

A handbook for teaching in the ghetto school

Come to a party given by parents for teachers and take in the panorama of cakes, chicken, and salad. Imagine the warmth of a handshake as a mother thanks a teacher for what he has done for her child.

Evaluate carefully the words of those teachers who say that the children can't learn or that the only way to make them behave is to hit them.

Visit a classroom where a teacher's softly modulated voice bespeaks a secure, stable, fruitful learning environment.

Peruse the newspaper records that tell of violence against whites and of student attacks against teachers.

Read Sylvia Ashton-Warner's *Teacher,* where she describes how she takes energies that could move toward destructiveness and channels them into areas that are beautifully creative. Study the following words of Erich Fromm: "Life has an inner dynamism of its own; it tends to grow, to be expressed, to be lived. The amount of destructiveness in a child is proportionate to the amount to which the expansiveness of his life has been curtailed. Destructiveness is the outcome of the unlived life."

Examine your feelings regarding teaching in the ghetto, your expectations about what school should be like, and your knowledge of the Negro as a minority group. Are you concerned about your ability to control the children, to reach them, and to teach them? Perhaps you see school as did E. R. Braithwaite, the author of *To Sir, With Love,* who wrote, "My vision of teaching in a school was one of straight rows of desks and neat, well-mannered obedient children." Are you able to see Negroes as people like yourself, people desiring acceptance, wanting to believe in the possible fulfillment of aspiration?

As teacher, you will be faced by some children who live in day-to-day contact with undesirable images; whose belongings are few and subject to confiscation by older, stronger boys; whose world is a mass of unfocused loud noise; who know instability as it comes from having a frequent change of step-fathers, from moving often, and from having different teachers within the same school year.

You will walk through streets that seem always strewn with litter. You will deal with some parents who are apathetic, some who are hostile, and some who passionately hope for a better life for their children.

You will hear the cynical remarks of some of your colleagues. You will be the target of broadside attacks by groups desiring to improve the quality of education in depressed-area schools. You will hear the warnings of friends and family who look askance at the foolish temerity of anyone daring to enter the reportedly violent atmosphere of a ghetto school.

The challenge is to provide stability in a world of chaos, to understand children some of whose values may be foreign to you, to help children accept themselves in spite of the burden of minority-group membership, and to expose your spirit to the feelings of the children that reach out for support and understanding.

The challenge is to look at the inner, personal core of your being, to bring out your fears and your attitudes. The challenge is to allow yourself to be caught up in a world that is changing. The challenge is to join the tide of that change which is hopefully moving toward a better education for all children, a melting of divisive barriers, and a more closely knit community.

The challenge is to see children as individuals. It is to recognize that not all children in the neighborhood come from depressed families. It is to realize that while some children come to school on cold winter days mostly because it's warm, others come with an avid desire to learn. It is to be aware that while some families isolate their children as best they can from the community, others dismiss them into the disordered world of the streets. It is to see that while some children have made a

poor adjustment (they are either too aggressive or too with-
drawn), others adjust very well.

The challenge is to relate to the parents and children in a
way that communicates interest, that commands respect, and
that convinces that school success is possible.

The challenge is to provide a curriculum that achieves participation on the part of the children and does not repeat patterns
of failure.

The challenge is to find those instructional materials from
which children can learn.

The challenge is to play your part in a revolution of which
education is a significant part.

Perhaps the challenge is as Langston Hughes, the Negro poet
laureate, puts it in his poem "Esthete in Harlem":

> Strange
> That in this nigger place
> I should meet life face to face
> When for years, I had been seeking
> Life in places gentler-speaking
> Until I came to this vile street
> And found Life stepping on my feet.

SOURCES OF GRATIFICATION

With a challenge that looms so large, why then should a teacher
want to enter schools that are different and beset by tension,
that shatter myths of model classrooms, and that—sometimes
harshly—bring a teacher face to face with himself? Teachers
in these schools reply:

"Other children may learn even without a teacher. Here the
teacher is responsible for so much of what the children learn."

"Here the teacher is needed."

"Children who have changed for the better make you feel
a sense of accomplishment."

20

What is the world I enter?

"You feel responsible for helping a child to make it."

"I feel more like a man because I've been dealing with a situation that takes a man. Immaturity won't do."

"I'm on the inside of real excitement. I know about things here in Harlem from firsthand knowledge."

"I see the children grow."

"I feel good coming to Harlem. We've got to come back to our people. I've made it but I've come back. I see a child doing well because of something I did."

The words of ex-students have given teachers cause for satisfaction. A graduate who returned to talk to a former teacher illustrated this when he said: "You cared about us. You made us behave. We could have done some terrible things. If I hadn't known that you tried so hard to make us to be gentlemen, I probably wouldn't be in school today."

James Baldwin expressed a similar idea: "There was a white teacher who became interested in me and took me to a play downtown. I became interested in the theater."

Perhaps the most significant source of gratification may be in joining the struggle to rectify the wrongs of decades. A rabbi speaking during the 1963 March on Washington spoke of this, in a way, when he said in essence, "The worst crime of humanity is silence in the face of oppression."

The teacher need not be a silent bystander as the Negro seeks to throw off the burden of prejudice and discrimination. He can participate in laying the groundwork for an improved generation. He can have a direct effect on the lives of children. He can learn about himself more quickly and more clearly than if he remained in the parochial world of his own familiar surroundings. He can bring meaning to his own existence.

2 How can I make it with the kids?

Many new teachers in ghetto elementary schools are disappointed when they find they cannot develop a good classroom atmosphere for learning. They resort to punitive techniques of which they do not approve and which, in addition, are only temporarily inhibiting. An examination of the reasons for this failure and a look at the approaches of those teachers who have succeeded in making contact with the children may help new teachers create an educational environment in which children adhere to standards and apply themselves academically.

CAUSES OF DIFFICULTY

There are three major causes of difficulty: one is the area of expectation patterns; another is a failure to recognize the importance of routines and how to establish them; a third is the personal fears of new teachers entering a cultural framework that is totally strange to them. Successful teachers have commented on these problem areas:

"Some new teachers don't give the children enough credit for being able to stick to rules and regulations."

"The teacher comes in expecting trouble."

"The controls of new teachers are lacking."

"They don't understand the importance of routines."

"Some teachers are afraid of the children. They're even afraid to handle a child's pencil. They hear a stick crack as they walk the streets in the neighborhood and they jump."

Expectations are part of everyone's personality. We travel to France and we anticipate eating good food. We visit Puerto Rico and we expect to hear Spanish spoken. We read stories of violence and we expect violence. We see such films as *The Blackboard Jungle* and we expect chaotic classrooms. We peruse sensational news reports of student attacks on teachers and we expect this form of behavior to be the norm.

The successful teacher either has no abnormal expectations to start with or has found that bizarre behavior is just that— unusual rather than typical. He has learned through direct experience, through reading, and through self-examination that children in depressed-area elementary schools are in many respects like all other children. He has become aware of the ways in which they are different, so that when these differences show themselves he is not shocked into inaction. He has learned about the backgrounds, the values, and the aspirations of the children. He reads Negro newspapers and magazines, such as the *New York Amsterdam News, Ebony,* and *Freedomways;* he has read the sociological treatises of Myrdal, Frazier, and Handlin; he has read the more personal reminiscences of Roi Ottley, Claude Brown, and James Baldwin.

A handbook for teaching in the ghetto school

Listen to successful teachers who have exposed themselves to direct experiences:

"I took a tour of the neighborhood to check on what I'd read. I tried to relate what I saw to the children in my class. I still take periodic tours to see what's happening."

"My mother works in the junior high school across the street. I used to visit her. Some of the children came to our home."

"My first years here I went into the homes of all the children in my class. You can see for yourself. Many of the children live in such crowded conditions that there isn't even a hook to hang your coat on. There isn't even a place to put a book."

"I worked with the kids as part of a college course. I saw them in play areas, in school, with their families. I began to understand the things they like, their fears, their difficulties at home."

A teacher who is mature and has learned about the children does not have lowered expectations, yet still can deal with atypical occurrences in an understanding manner. He can say, as one teacher said: "The children don't do things because they don't like the teacher. It's a way of getting rid of hurts." This type of teacher is not stunned by the morality of a child who has found a nickel and refuses to return it to its original owner. He understands the child's insistence about stating the community's law of possession. Rather than condemning the child who says, "What I found and I have is mine," he sees it as another opportunity to teach. This kind of teacher is not shocked by profanity but rather teaches that the word is unacceptable in school. This type of teacher doesn't take things for granted. For example, he realizes that for many of the children recreation is almost entirely of the "free play" variety. Mothers say, "Go out and play," and children do not learn about sportsmanship, about how to play organized games, or about taking turns. This type of teacher doesn't denounce the family milieu because there are so many one-parent homes and large families. Rather,

24

he understands from reading such books as Frazier's *The Negro Family in the United States* how a matriarchial family structure developed from roots in a slave society.

The successful teacher understands the sources of the children's problems and yet maintains standards. This is illustrated by the teacher who said: "When a child comes to school one day and has difficulty functioning, I know there's a reason why. There may have been drinking at home, or the television set has been blaring until late at night, or he hasn't eaten anything or a hundred other reasons. But I can't stop at the problem, I work with the problem. I try to alleviate it. But no matter what, I'm going to teach him."

THE NEED FOR STRUCTURE

The teacher who is successful in ghetto areas clearly defines limits and shows his respect and liking for the children by indicating his belief in their ability to adhere to standards and by his insistence that they do so. Teacher after teacher has stated this maxim, each in his own way.

"I set up routines carefully. I let the children know what's expected. Standards are within reach and maybe a little beyond, so there's some place to go. I brook no leeway."

"If you insist on the regulations, the children will live up to them."

"Everyone knows what they have to do from the word 'Go.' "

"The children know what they can expect from the start."

Redl and Wineman in their book *Controls from Within,* lend substantiation to the concept that clear routine has value: "A certain amount of routinization under certain conditions, even where not needed for reasons of expediency or administrative smoothness, may have the value of increasing the total security of the child."

Louis Heil reports on research which indicates that "a school

A handbook for teaching in the ghetto school

with a high incidence of opposing and anxious children should have a relatively large proportion of teachers whose personality characteristics will help create a high degree of structure and order, with emphasis on setting immediate goals."

Structure is the clarification of the relationship between behavior and consequences. Specifically the term refers to the following:

1. setting up definite and dependable classroom routines;

2. giving at first very specific and limited tasks, which later can be extended and embellished as the child's emotional self-control and educational application increases; and

3. remaining consistent and following through on requirements until they are reasonably fulfilled.

All of this implies an awareness on the part of the teacher of how much emotional self-control the children have and what routines need teaching. The teacher who develops a firm structure works with the children on routines for their leaving the lavatory, using the pencil sharpener, walking through the corridors, entering the classroom, saluting the flag, participating in fire drills, distributing books and materials, doing homework, getting clothing, changing seats for group instruction, collecting money, caring for books, maintaining the appearance of the room, and all the other tasks that make up the structure of the school and class world.

Illustrations of the children's desire for clear expectation patterns abound. One teacher made it a daily habit to stand at the classroom door and say "Good Morning" to each child as he or she entered the room. Once the teacher became momentarily involved in answering the question of another teacher; a child reminded her that she had forgotten to extend her daily greeting to him.

Other teachers emphasize the desirability of structure. One teacher says: "It's so crazy in their homes that I want to settle them down as soon as they enter class. When they come in first thing in the morning, there's always work for them to do on the blackboard. They look forward to it. Once I neglected to place the assignment on the board and the children reminded me of it."

Another teacher put it this way: "There's a place for every single thing. If I change something, I'll let the children know."

The teacher's daily presence is an extremely important part of the security pattern of the child. One child reacted to his teacher's absence by saying, "I heard I was going to have a substitute and I got so mad I didn't know what I was doing."

USE OF REWARDS

To gain adherence to routine and to promote habits of acceptable school behavior, successful teachers make use of some form of recognition. They are alert for opportunities to praise, and they sometimes make use of extrinsic rewards. Such an approach is worthwhile if it gives the children satisfying experiences which will make them want to be involved in positive school activity.

One teacher indicated the value of outside recognition by saying: "The use of extrinsic motivation helps. We have a tendency to notice the bad. Giving rewards helps the teacher to emphasize the good."

That the immediate satisfaction of rewards is important for lower-class children is attested to by Allison Davis and John Dollard in their book *Children of Bondage,* when they say, "If there is no reward for learning, in terms of privilege and anxiety-reduction, there is no motive for work."

Leonard Kornberg, in his *Class for Disturbed Children,* also indicates the values to be gained from some form of outside recognition. He remarks: "I utilized opportunities to feed the narcissistic qualities of children through marks, report cards, individualized progress charts, the stimulation of visitors to the room, and through bulletin board displays of the children's work."

THE IMPORTANCE OF CLASSROOM ORGANIZATION

The classroom itself can take on special importance for children who have had little in their lives in the way of physical surroundings to which they could lay personal claim. The successful teacher recognizes that the classroom is a way of talking to children without words. The teacher who is fastidious and systematic about room cleanliness may be showing greater interest in children than would many words of exhortation and protestation. This type of teacher realizes that an attractively decorated and organized room gives children experience with a place that encourages respect and care. Teacher after teacher has reported the pride children take in the appearance of their classroom, a pride that is evidenced by the enjoyment they show as they guide visitors around the room. The use of colorful pictures, including some which show Negro subjects, can help give the children a personal identity with their surroundings. The teacher who periodically changes room displays can help to keep children curious. An attractive room is an offering by the teacher to the children.

The successful teacher encourages the idea that the room belongs to the children. One teacher worked toward the development of this feeling by placing a box of pencils on his desk to which the children were free to help themselves. He reported that the pencils were borrowed and almost invariably returned the next day.

Observation of successful teachers revealed their awareness of the importance of giving recognition, creating an ordered

28

environment, appealing to the visual and tactile senses of the children, and developing an attractive atmosphere. All of their rooms included displays of the children's work. Some portion of the class bulletin board space was devoted to samples of the children's art work, their written expression, spelling papers, and mathematics papers. The delegation of classroom responsibilities was invariably listed and displayed in a colorful manner, thereby giving recognition to the children. Charts entitled "Class Helpers," "Helping Hands," "Class Duties," or "Class Officers" were found in every room.

The organizational ability and neatness of successful teachers were evident upon entering their rooms. All the bulletin boards were neatly backed with colored paper. Each tack and staple was in place; not a paper was askew. The children's papers had been neatly folded and headed. Schedules of class activities were clearly visible. It was interesting to see that bars of soap and cleaning powder were available at almost every sink. There were captions and labels for pictures and area centers. It was apparent that these rooms were lived in by people for whom an ordered attractiveness was important.

Part of the room organization was an appeal to the visual and tactile senses of the children. There were colorful pictures neatly mounted, maps of the school and community, magnets, prisms, rock collections, flower and leaf displays, rhythm instruments, clocks, scales, dry cells, wire, flashlights, puzzles, toys, and word games. Living things were present in the form of plants, fish in aquariums, and vegetation in terrariums.

Experience charts were written in a clear, neat hand. Bulletin boards were headed by questions designed to catch children's interest. Materials relating to the various subject areas were displayed on separate bulletin boards. The children's free time was planned for by such charts as the one entitled "When I Finish My Work I Can . . ."

Children contributed to the organization of the room by suggesting and bringing in items which helped to make the room more attractive. Often they suggested the best locations for library materials and science displays. They brought in plants, sewed curtains, and designed seasonal decorations. Some of the teachers set aside bulletin boards which the children planned and developed themselves. With the guidance of the teacher they learned the importance of color coordination, balance, design, and effective labeling. In this manner they not only developed a sense of pride in their room but also learned what they could do to make their surroundings at home more attractive.

DEALING WITH FAILURE

Many of the children in depressed-area schools have had repeated experience with failure. The successful teacher recognizes the need for modifying the child's previous educational environment to emphasize what is wholesome and constructive in the child's makeup. He knows that he must convince children of their ability to achieve. Rather than allowing himself to be overwhelmed by a child's apparent weaknesses, be they in the area of academic achievement or emotional growth, the successful teacher learns to recognize, value, and develop the unique individual strengths possessed by each child.

One teacher reported the example of a child who was a behavior problem but who, he discovered, was the best bongo player in the class. There are other children with academic weaknesses who can make their contributions to the class through art work, athletic ability, a sense of humor, and reports of interests in such hobbies as weight-lifting. Making use of such abilities can help to improve self-esteem and lead in time to greater academic achievement.

30

How can I make it with the kids?

One teacher described her approach this way: "I know that for many children school has been one big flop. I look for chances for children to contribute. If a child knows a song or a poem or a story, I let him present it. If a child just seems as though he has something to say, I let him say it. I try to make them feel good about themselves."

For children who are all too familiar with failure, teachers have tried to arrange matters so that they can master the school environment. One teacher found that with a group of slow children he was able to do this, at least in the initial stages, by providing them with simple, rote activity, usually arithmetic computation. Particularly with slower children, teachers have found that graded workbooks are useful because they provide clearly defined tasks which can be geared to ability.

A teacher explained his method with slow children as follows:

> These are kids who are deathly afraid of school work. They feel they can't do it, that they'll be laughed at, or that they'll be marked as dumb. It helps when you encourage them and when you accept what they have to offer. For example, when they write or tell stories, I emphasize their ideas and not their spelling or grammar. After a while the ideas begin to flow, and they've got some good ones.

Another teacher indicated his manner of dealing with children with a history of failure by saying:

> I try to work with them in a way that won't remind them of their failure. For example, I don't rely very much on the basal reader to teach reading. They just haven't learned to read that way. Instead I work with filmstrips, music, and experience charts. I use storybooks, SRA material, and *Reader's Digest* skill builders to teach reading. The children are more likely to use these materials without any memory of failure.

Some teachers found that using the i/t/a (initial teaching

31

alphabet) media in teaching reading has been of great value in working with children who were previously unsuccessful in learning to read. Many of these children become fascinated with the new method of decoding words as represented by the i/t/a. As one teacher put it: "Look, if they haven't learned to read any other way, we've got to try something different. I/t/a is fun for them. It becomes a game to use this new code. It helps a lot of the children who have failed with other approaches to reading."

Other teachers planned opportunities for individual contact. One teacher said: "I am not aloof. I try to give each child a few minutes every day." The teacher who gives individual attention to a child who is having learning difficulty is telling the child that when he makes a mistake, adults don't necessarily punish or reject but stand by to help. The trouble a teacher takes indicates to the child that he is important. And the teacher who helps the child to find the answer himself is expressing confidence in the child and declaring to him that he has a basis for respecting his own ability.

TYPICAL FORMS OF MISBEHAVIOR

The new teacher must realize that at some time he may be defied, he may see fighting, and he may hear profanity. His aim at these times should be to deal realistically with deviations from acceptable school behavior, to examine the reasons for the deviations, and to handle his own reactions. Louis Harper and Benjamin Wright, in *The Exceptional Child,* indicate the special importance of this last point: "The teacher has to manage his own feelings in times of stress, so that he does not require his emotional energy himself. Only if he is relatively free from a preoccupation with his own needs will the teacher be able to remain sensitive to the child's needs and to help the child."

32

How can I make it with the kids?

Defiance. There are deviations from acceptable school behavior which every teacher in a ghetto elementary school faces at one time or another. An understanding of the possible reasons for the behavior can aid the teacher in dealing with it. For example, there is the child who says, teeth gritted in defiance, "I won't take my sweater off." He refuses despite demands, pleas, cajoling, or threats by the teacher.

A private discussion with the child can reveal the reasons for this refusal. It may be that underneath the sweater the child wears a shirt that is torn or is without three or four buttons. In that case reason dictates that the child be allowed to keep the sweater on. Perhaps the reason for the defiance is that the sweater represents a new possession for the child, and he is reluctant to let it out of his sight for fear that it will fall to the floor and be stepped on. Teachers have handled this sort of case in a number of ways. They have reassured the child about the sweater's safety in the closet; they have allowed the child to hold it at his desk; they have permitted the child to continue wearing it; or they have carefully placed it in their own closet.

One teacher described how she deals with the situation: "I tell the child I can understand his concern about the sweater. I like to take good care of my things, too. I demonstrate for the children how to fold a sweater for placement on a shelf such as the one in the wardrobe. Then I have a few children practice folding the sweater properly."

Teachers indicate that the most effective course of action in dealing with defiance is to handle it calmly in private, and by looking at the possible causes for such behavior.

Fighting. Fighting occurs often enough in some classes for the teacher to moan, as one did, "Sometimes I feel like a referee." The reasons for fighting are not difficult to uncover. When children grow up in neighborhoods and homes where aggressive behavior is the approved way of dealing with difficulty, fighting often occurs. When children see adults using this method to settle problems, they may very likely imitate them. When children have had to use fighting as a means of self-protection, it is not surprising that they adopt it as a method for dealing with trouble in school.

Fights break out for other reasons as well. The high rate of pupil mobility in ghetto elementary schools adds to the number of fights that take place. A bid to test out a new member of the class group may be an invitation to fight. Teachers sometimes contribute to this neg..tive approach by their own reactions to the newcomer. When a teacher finds himself overwhelmed by a constantly changing and enlarging register, he may greet the newcomer with a grimace rather than a smile. Teachers who are aware of the frequency of newcomers to the class can plan to deal with the problem by preparing programs of welcome. This may lead to an internalization of the teacher's reaction by the children and diminish the likelihood of fights.

The outside playground of the school during the lunch hour is the scene of many battles between children. The noise and furor of free play is too much for some children. They are overstimulated by the turmoil of the activity and become involved in pushing and shoving that lead to fights. Quiet areas, such as the library or classrooms open during lunchtime, for children to work with puzzles and other quieting material, can help children gain respite from the chaos of the playground. Another alternative is to organize games and other forms of physical activity under the supervision of older children or adult volunteers.

Teachers have attempted to deal with the problem of fighting in various ways. One teacher said: "When I greet the children at the door in the morning, I can quickly sense who has already had a pretty tough start to the day. I provide something for him to do or give him some sort of attention. A kind word can help."

Another teacher indicated an approach she used by saying: "Role-playing a fighting situation can help. The children learn something about what causes fights. They begin to learn about other ways for dealing with differences."

A third teacher remarked: "I let them talk about the things that bother them. Talking about them helps to get rid of the anger."

Another teacher noted: "Cooling off is what a fight needs. When a fight occurs—and they happen less often now that the children know me and each other—I separate the children and give them a chance to relax. Then we talk about it."

Still another teacher said: "I show respect for a child's right to be angry. When he's been hit by another child or his book has been torn, I support his right to be angry. But I point out to him that fighting in class stops everyone else from learning. I assure him that the wrong he has experienced will be taken care of."

The greatest deterrent to fights in the classroom is an atmosphere in which children are involved in satisfying activity, feel the security of clear expectation patterns, are exposed to a controlled set of stimuli, and feel a strong identity with the teacher.

Tattling. The child who tattles constantly represents a gadfly for many teachers. But if the teacher recognizes that some children are embroiled in a constant effort to stay out of trouble, to check their impulses, he may understand that the child who is forever tattling may be seeking approbation and assurance that he can restrain himself from participating in misbehavior. The struggle to resist is clearly illustrated by the child who wants to sit alone, away from the other children who may be the targets of his impulses. The inner disturbance of other children is exemplified by the child who said: "Please don't send me to that room. It's too quiet there. It makes me nervous." This child may have needed exterior noise to quell the sound of inner turmoil.

Teachers have sought to diminish tattling by giving credit

35

A handbook for teaching in the ghetto school

for adherence to school and class codes of behavior. The teacher may also indicate to the child who constantly reports on others that, although he is pleased that the child is not involved in the deviant act, there is no need to tell about other children.

Lying. Teachers have complained about children who fail to take responsibility for their actions and resort to lying. Some children may have learned about lying from seeing adults use this approach. The parent who lies to evade the very personal probing of welfare investigators, social workers, or rent collectors gives the child a very vivid model to follow. In low socioeconomic areas where many parents commonly use a punitive approach to deal with infractions, children may lie rather than expose themselves to harsh punishment. Here, too, the teacher must study the total situation to which the behavior is a response. If the child is lying to escape a situation which seems dangerous to him, the teacher can try to alleviate the danger through discussion with the parent, or attempt to avoid placing the child in a position where lying appears to be his only recourse. If the child is lying to achieve status or security, then other responses are in order. For example, some children in Harlem elementary schools have made up stories about fathers at home where none has existed. The most sensible response, in this case, is for the teacher to recognize the reason and to accept the fantasy, at least for the moment. Other children may lie because in their immaturity they mix fact and fiction. The causes of lying determine the teacher's action.

Stealing. One way to counteract stealing is to avoid tempting a child. Children will sometimes indirectly indicate to the teacher that they are tempted. For example, children have made such remarks to teachers as:

"Don't leave your money on the desk. Somebody might take it."

"You'd better put your wallet in another place. It's easy to pull out of your pocket now."

36

How can I make it with the kids?

The teacher who places money or candy in easy reach of the child who is having a difficult time restraining impulses is being unfair to him.

Sometimes children take things to explore the properties of these objects. One group of children under the supervision of an ineffective substitute teacher helped themselves to recorders and song flutes. When it was explained that this act deprived other children of music lessons and that return of the instruments would involve no punishment, the children returned the instruments. The lesson here was that the instruments should not have been so easily available, and that the theft was based more on curiosity than anything else. In dealing with stealing it is futile to decide on any one course of action before the causes of the deviant behavior are carefully examined.

Profanity. Epithets and obscenities are often the signal for angry looks that lead to angry blows. "He called my mother a name" is the reason frequently given the teacher as the cause of a fight. When the teacher notes that the child with the most disoriented kind of mother-child relationship is often the quickest to take umbrage at such a slight he can understand better that this child may be reacting to guilt about his own antagonistic feelings toward his mother. The teacher can, in this instance, agree with the child who feels the insult that such language is unacceptable and assure him of his plans to stop it. Such assurance can succeed in warding off blows and help in assuaging the child's guilt.

If the use of obscene language is handled without shock or anger, it is unlikely that a child will come to feel that such language is a weapon that he can use against the "grownup" world. If the language is used out of ignorance of its inappropriateness, then teaching is in order. If the obscene language is the result of an outburst of anger, then the anger needs to be dealt with. To use threats as a means of stamping out the obscene language is to lend status to a forbidden act. When chil-

37

dren identify with the teacher and are made aware of the inappropriateness of obscene language for the classroom, then the use of such language is minimal.

Restlessness. "Some of the children are so restless" is the plaintive cry of many new teachers in the ghetto. In order to deal with this problem it is once again necessary to pose questions. Why are the children acting restless? What are possible ways of dealing with the problem? What effect will the selected method have on the class? If the hyperactivity of the child or children is due to physical cause, then medical attention is called for. If the child is seeking to break class rules as a means of gaining status, then a firm authoritative command may be in order. If restlessness is general and due to boredom, then a change of activity is advised.

In any case, the successful teacher intersperses physical activities with academic tasks. He has a knowledge of games, arts and crafts activities, dramatization materials, and songs which will permit frequent opportunities for children to release physical energy. He knows the value of involving children directly in the performing of such academic tasks as conducting science experiments, figuring mathematical problems, and studying the lives of great men. For example, children can handle simple equipment in science demonstrations; they can use the blackboard and manipulate materials to solve mathematical problems; they can act out stories which depict events in the lives of people who have contributed to the development of our country.

Teachers have indicated the need to be sensitive to the staying capacity of the children and not to permit activities to continue beyond the attention span of the class. One teacher described it this way: "I've learned that my children can concentrate on a particular activity for about twenty minutes. After that time I change to something else. With each new class one of the first things I do is try to get the feel of how long the children can stick to something."

Since ghetto elementary schoolchildren live in a world that is active and surrounded by noise, the teacher can plan his program to include controlled physical activity and to provide a balance between the physical and the sedentary.

Truancy. Truancy is not a normal occurrence. Like most negative acts, the causes of truancy can be multiple in nature. Sometimes the truancy may be a result of continued failure in school. There have been other instances where a child's adjustment in school has been better than in any of his other areas of living, and yet he is truant. The cause here may likely be a disoriented family situation in which the child uses truancy to vent his anger toward a parent or parents who have neglected or mistreated him. Traumatic incidents have resulted in truancy. One child accidentally struck his teacher as she attempted to break up a fight in which he was involved. This so unnerved him that he became truant from school. On occasion children have been detained at home by parents who, because of other pressures or because of irresponsibility, have assigned them to watch over younger brothers and sisters. Children have missed school because they lacked clothing or shoes. In these cases it is possible to refer the parents to the district attendance bureau which very often maintains both a Shoe Fund and Overcoat Fund.

In most elementary schools teachers follow through on truancy by sending postcards to the family and by filling out truant slips for attendance officers to investigate. Although this procedure provides some communication between home and school, more intensive work is required to counter the problem of truancy. Children need to feel a sense of accomplishment and acceptance in school. They need to be part of a family configuration where interchange of feeling is allowed.

A handbook for teaching in the ghetto school

Chronic truancy calls for the cooperative efforts of teachers, guidance counselors, the school administration, the home, and social agencies to study the situation in depth and to focus on ameliorating the factors that contribute to a child's seeking escape from school.

Since many children in low socioeconomic areas resist authority, teachers in these schools are more likely to encounter behavior that violates school norms. But if teachers understand the environmental factors that contribute to this type of behavior, they can deal with deviations more effectively and decrease classroom conflicts. The principle underlying this approach is supported by the results of an experimental study conducted by Frances Wilkinson and Ralph Ojemann. The data they obtained showed that learning becomes more effective and the development of personality can be more adequately controlled if a careful analysis of children's behavior is made by the teacher.

The teachers who succeed in making contact with children do not condone any and all actions. Rather they try to understand why children act as they do for guides to intelligent and effective ways of dealing with deviation.

3 How do they do it?

There are teachers in the ghetto who walk the same blocks from the subway to school each day, bodies rigid, eyes staring straight ahead as if fearful of touching unpleasantness. They enter their classrooms like fighters entering a boxing ring, ready to defend themselves, ready to counterattack.

The teachers who meet with success are those who stop to buy sodas or packs of cigarettes at the corner candy store, who telephone or visit children who are ill, who place their summer addresses on the blackboard for children to write to them, who don't react to the child who struts into the room with belligerent feelings of his own, and who don't feel personally affronted by children who deviate from class standards.

The teachers who succeed in helping the children to achieve

and to develop wholesome school attitudes are in depressed-area schools because it is where they want to teach. Among the teachers interviewed for this study is one who travels each day from New Jersey, another who commutes from Connecticut, another who did her student teaching in a special elementary school for gifted children but preferred to start her teaching career in Harlem, and another who came from another state seeking a teaching position in Harlem. They are unlike teachers who, in constant search of applause, see themselves as martyrs or saints carrying the message of civilization to a poor underprivileged minority. They understand that such an attitude breeds resentment and feelings such as those described by Thoreau when he gave his reaction to the potential missionary of good will: "If I knew for a certainty that a man was coming to my house with the conscious design of doing me good, I should run for my life for fear that I should get some of his good done to me, some of its virus mingled with my blood."

Successful teachers are also open with the children regarding their own feelings. As one teacher said: "A teacher in a ghetto neighborhood has to develop the capacity to accept his own human feelings and to express them if need be. The children don't expect you to be godlike."

Another teacher stated: "I make no bones about expressing my own deep feelings."

A third remarked: "I'm not reluctant to let children know how I feel about a situation. I'll explain my own feelings to the children if I think it's appropriate."

These are teachers who overtly display their lack of fear and their acceptance and liking for the children. One teacher put it this way: "I never sit at my desk teaching. I get in with the children. I move around the room. You don't sit in one spot and teach. Everything they do I get in and do with them. I

42

jump rope with them. I sit at their desks and help them with math problems."

These teachers succeed in extending the rigid boundary of the nine-to-three classrooms by having personal friends visit the school. One teacher asked a musician acquaintance to demonstrate his talents; another teacher had a journalist friend describe his work and tell the children about some of the skills needed for his profession; a folk singer was the guest of another teacher. These teachers have brought personal items to class. One brought his camera to school to take pictures of the children's art work. Another showed photographs of his dog when the class was discussing pets. Other teachers have brought collections of sea shells to class, have loaned personal books to the children, and have brought phonograph records from home for the children to hear.

Successful teachers in ghetto schools reach beyond the normal, everyday routine of teaching. One teacher took the children to the library after three o'clock. Another escorted children on a Saturday trip to a puppet show. She reported the amazement of the children that someone had come on a Saturday to take them someplace. Another group of teachers in one Harlem school met with some of the parents over the summer in one of the teacher's homes to work out cooperatively an approach to school problems. The very act of giving time converted what had been an angry group of parents into a group convinced of teacher commitment and eager to cooperate. Other teachers have invited their relatives to attend a class play or to accompany the class on a trip.

A trait common to these teachers is their ability to look at the deplorable and even bizarre backgrounds of some of the children without a dramatic expression of sorrow. They do not show themselves as people who pry or who are prim and prissy. Because of these qualities they can ask a child if he has had

43

A handbook for teaching in the ghetto school

any breakfast and get a truthful response. Then, if necessary, arrangements can be made for the child to get something to eat without any embarrassment. One teacher, in order to help teach the children better dietary habits and to aid them in starting the day on a better footing, formed a breakfast club. The teacher and children breakfasted on dry cereal, milk, and fruit.

Of course, the teacher in the ghetto must avoid the pitfall of assuming he must take over all parental responsibilities. For example, one parent objected strenuously to the offer of a school to pay for her child's eyeglasses with the angry words, "I can afford to buy my child glasses. I earn a living. I don't need your help." In addition, for the school to take over the parent's role totally may retard parental growth and emasculate the family as a source of support for the child. Successful teachers realize the limits of the support they can offer.

These teachers also reveal a sincere interest in the children and in their out-of-school activities. One teacher shows this interest by noticing a library book a child is holding and asking him about it. Other teachers provide time during the school day for children to talk about their hobbies. Another teacher displays his concern by taking a child to a nearby dental clinic to care for a throbbing toothache. At school and class parties time is allotted to dances the children enjoy. The teacher reveals her interest in such dances as the Wobble, the Drunken Sailor, and the Monkey by asking the children to teach her the steps. For other teachers the end of the school year doesn't make for a sudden termination of their relationship with the children. One teacher indicated this idea in the following way: "I tell the children that I want to hear about how they are doing, that I'm available if they want to talk about anything that is bothering them. During the school year I make it my business to ask them how they are getting along."

Many of the teachers interviewed said that when they were interested in something, the children were interested; when they were enthusiastic, the children became enthusiastic; when they enjoyed what they were teaching, the children enjoyed it; and when they were excited over something, the children were also excited.

A teacher expressed it this way: "If I come to school tired, the children sense my lack of vitality and they get lethargic. On the other hand, when I'm full of life, when my eyes light up, they get excited, too. I've also learned to use my voice in an animated way. The children respond to a teacher who can be dramatic."

A child implied the same idea when he indicated his positive reaction to his teacher by saying of her, "She has life to teach."

An example of teacher interest, enthusiasm, enjoyment, and excitement getting across to the children is the class that became interested in Greek mythology because a teacher of Greek ancestry made a practice of reading Greek myths to them, bringing Greek artifacts to class, and speaking of the origin of her name and family. Or the group of children who began to understand more clearly the value of education because of the conviction and sincerity of their teacher (a Negro in this case), who stressed continually that opportunities for Negroes are opening up and that the children must be prepared to qualify for these opportunities. Or the teacher who showed her enjoyment of music by bringing her guitar to class, singing with the children, helping the children learn to play the song flute, and developing a repertoire of songs with them.

These teachers know that who they are and what they know can influence the learning process. They realize that a textbook, a filmstrip, or a television program contributes to classroom learning only to the extent that the teacher does something with it. So they say, as one teacher did, "I never teach anything from a textbook unless I know a great deal more." They use their own strengths and interests to modify the curriculum.

Another approach that has proved effective with children

in ghetto elementary schools is the personalization of subject matter. For example, a teacher working on developing good speech took the actual sentences children had spoken, had them copied, and then focused attention on the errors and substituted the correct speech pattern. Another teacher in teaching about alphabetization had the children make up a class directory of their names and addresses. In helping children learn to write verbal descriptions, a teacher had the children write descriptions of others in the class. In making up problems in mathematics, teachers have used, in addition to realistic classroom situations, the names of children in the class to represent the people in the problems. Experience charts have given teachers numerous opportunities to personalize reading matter. Children contribute ideas and write them on a chart with a black magic marker. Then credit for the idea is given by writing the child's name in red next to his words. In other cases individual stories are dictated by children and recorded by the teacher to make up personal reading matter for the child.

Teachers who have succeeded in making contact with ghetto-area elementary schoolchildren present a picture of organization and of control. For example, their punctuality records show that they almost always reach school well in advance of the school day. The numerous school reports are handed in punctually. Their classrooms reveal a meticulousness that carries through to the last tack on the last corner of a child's posted drawing. This sense of organization and control is even communicated by the neatness of their dress. Just as each thing is in its place in the classroom, these teachers show in their grooming a concern for ordered attractiveness. They do not move into the day in a helter-skelter way but rather in a manner indicating that they know where they have come, what they have to do, and what they want to do.

Their planning is detailed and specific. It includes activities which are landmarks for the week, such as quiet seat work for the first thing in the morning and afternoon, and a reading lesson to initiate the formal start of the class's learning activities. Their planning also includes methods for clearly delineating class standards, for emphasizing these standards, and for evaluating them.

These teachers also display an almost phenomenal ability to recognize necessary routines, to analyze them in order to give the appropriate series of directions, and to concentrate on them day after day to make certain they are carried out successfully. They do not see working on these routines as menial drudgery but rather as steps in building a stable, secure world for children who in the face of disorder may become frightened and confused.

Yet none of these teachers operates with a single, inflexible approach:

"I'm forever learning from the children. When they don't listen, I look at the lesson to see what was wrong. The children make me active, make me think about the way I present things."

"I'm constantly reminding myself that not everything always has to be perfect. If something goes wrong I work at correcting it, and I don't consider that a major catastrophe has occurred."

"I use textbooks experimentally. I watch to see how they connect. If they don't, I'll have them changed for another set of books."

A capsule description of successful teachers in depressed-area elementary schools might therefore include the words unafraid, expressive, involved, accepting, vital, organized, and flexible. Perhaps a more graphic view of these characteristics can be presented by illustrating the case of one teacher who started his career in a school in the ghetto under extremely difficult conditions and managed to convert a totally disordered situation into one where children worked and learned. Perhaps such a description will offer a clearer picture of what it was that helped this teacher to achieve success.

THE STORY OF A NEW TEACHER

The month is February. Winter's cold has driven many of the neighborhood's jobless from the street corners and the stoops. Still there are groups of men looking for something to do, something to sustain them. The streets have a drearier, dirtier look than usual; discarded newspapers and bags are tossed chaotically from curb to curb by an ever-shifting wind.

Inside the five-story, seventy-year-old school building a group of sixth-grade children has been without a regular teacher since the beginning of the month. Each day the fourteen boys and five girls who comprise this slow sixth-grade class have climbed the winding staircases to the fifth floor and walked the narrow corridors to their classroom to await the *per diem* substitute who has been assigned to them—or, in the event that no substitute is available, to be broken into groups of three or four for placement in other classes.

With each passing day the class's group feeling has withered more. Children fail to bring their pencils and books. Some, in fits of anger or despair, leave their room to wander the halls or come to the office of the assistant principal for help, for some support, exactly what kind they don't know. Other children bedevil the substitute to allow them to use the class nok-hockey set. In the classroom a few remaining papers hang helplessly from the bulletin boards. Broken bits of crayon and pieces of paper are strewn over the floor.

On those days when the children are placed in other classes they are met with such remarks as: "When are they going to get a teacher?" "They'd better behave in here or they can't stay." Some of the children who hear that they are going to be broken up for the day just leave the building not to return. Others roam the halls until they are found and escorted to a room. There are some who leave their assigned class and return

48

to their old room to sit quietly at a desk thumbing through the pages of a book, to play with the nok-hockey set, or just to sit and talk.

Every day now children walk over to the assistant principal and plaintively ask, "When are we going to get a teacher?"

At the end of February a teacher is found. He is the brother of a woman teacher in the school. He has passed an emergency examination for a substitute license to teach in the elementary school. His college program had prepared him to teach English in the junior high school. He arrives February 27, neatly groomed, young, vigorous.

The teacher hears about his class. The assistant principal met with Mr. M. before he was to take over his class, to try to describe what had happened to the class this month without a regular teacher. As they talked, Mr. M. saw hallway stragglers from his class-to-be led to a classroom. A look at the cumulative record cards for the class showed that of the nineteen children all but one had previously been retained in a grade. The reading levels ranged from 3.2 to primer reading. Typical comments on the cards included the following:

"Truancy is a problem."

"You can't get his mother to come to school."

"He has frequent temper tantrums."

Other teachers also prepared Mr. M. for his class. When they were introduced to him by his sister, they responded with such remarks as: "You're in for a really rough time." "Why does your sister hate you so much?" "That class is absolutely wild."

Mr. M. described his introduction to the school: "Everyone thought I was crazy to take the class. They all hoped I'd stay because the kids were a nuisance to them, but they all described it as an impossible situation. The only people who had anything positive to say about the children were Mr. K. [a sixth-grade teacher] and the assistant principal. The kids were a lot more positive than any of the teachers. When they saw me in the hall, they'd ask me my name and if I were going to be their teacher. At the end of the day they'd want to know if I were going to be back the next day. I didn't realize it at the time, but they were grasping for someone."

The first days. Mr. M. had three days to become oriented to the school before he was actually to take the class. During this time visits were arranged to the classes of experienced teachers. One was the class of a teacher who was very strong in routines; another the class of a teacher who was skillful at organizing the curriculum; and the third was the class of a teacher whose soft, sympathetic manner maintained a wholesome class atmosphere.

Mr. M. spoke of these visits as follows:

"Visiting those classes helped a lot. No one made me think that any one approach would be better than another. I was just told I'd be seeing different approaches and to pick up on those things I thought I could use. I saw one teacher during a music lesson put her arm around a boy who had gotten out of his seat and guide him back. Another used her voice in a firm, strong way and that seemed to work for her. I got the feeling I'd have to develop my own style, the one that was right for me."

Meetings with the assistant principal were held daily to formulate aims, to take care of immediate needs, and to deal with questions. The two men decided that Mr. M.'s initial goals would be to reintroduce the children to an academic atmosphere, give them a sense of stability, and develop a sense of a class group. By concentrating on routines and working with a simple and specific curriculum, it was hoped that structure and stability would be achieved. Workbooks were provided as an aid to an inexperienced teacher in giving children simple, definite assignments. A literature series was chosen which contained stories of high interest and were on a low enough reading level to be used by all the children. Mr. M. was first introduced to spelling and handwriting methodology, because it was felt that the methodology in these areas would be simpler for him to handle. Because of the academic retardation of the class, the study-test method in spelling was decided upon rather than the test-study method.

As a means of instilling individual and class pride, all textbooks formerly held by the class were removed, and Mr. M. was prepared with new notebooks, new pencils, new workbooks, and new textbooks for his class.

Suggestions were made regarding planning. It was made clear that there would be no rigid curriculum to which Mr. M. would have to adhere. It was suggested, for example, that the construction of a new school, only a block away, might be used as a source of curriculum material. Experience charts and their possible use the first day in introducing the teacher and the new program were discussed.

There were many obvious disadvantages in the situation. But there were positive aspects as well. For one thing, there was the eagerness of the children to have a teacher. Secondly, the size of the group was small. One of the most important aids for Mr. M. was the contact provided him by the fact that his sister had already been teaching in the school. He described what this meant to him: "Having a sister who taught in the school helped more than I can say. Older teachers don't realize how difficult it is for a new person right out of college to walk into any working situation, let alone a teaching situation. When other teachers are cold and aloof, when they don't say hello, the new teacher feels left out, lost, bewildered by the social setup. For a new teacher, attending the first teachers' meeting or going into the teachers' cafeteria is a frightening experience. My sister introduced me to everyone, and the informal help I got was great. Teachers explained things, gave me materials. Most important, though, was the fact that I had heard talk from my sister at home. I had gone on trips with her class. One night I came home and she had brought a couple of kids home with her for dinner. Before I came here I knew something about the kids.

"Another thing was that my sister had a very positive attitude toward teaching here. She really enjoyed it. And besides I couldn't fail after my older sister had succeeded."

Other experiences helped prepare Mr. M. for his teaching in the ghetto. His work at the educational clinic of his college helped him to get ready for a difficult class. In describing this experience he said: "I worked with kids who had lots of trouble. The first time I heard a kid curse it threw me. Then, when it happened again, I dealt with it better. I had the experience of seeing what was for me bizarre behavior. In the clinic I'd let it go. In the class when the same things happened I didn't let them go but they didn't throw me."

In the classroom. Mr. M.'s start in the classroom was a combination of frustration, trauma, and learning. He described his initial meeting with the class as follows:

"The first day alone in the classroom I was so frightened it was amazing. And after each day for those first few weeks I can honestly say that I went home every afternoon muttering to myself that I wasn't coming back to that nonsense the next day. It used to take me until ten or eleven to unwind each night.

"I can remember trying to get the class down the stairway at three o'clock. It was unbelievable. They just wouldn't listen. They weren't hearing me. When I told them to stop at the landing, they ran around, they yelled things at me. They were out of the building before I knew it. I was just some guy up there saying some words. I said to myself, 'Hey, I'm your teacher.' I couldn't believe it. It was so frustrating. I didn't know what to do. I tried having them do it over. I tried keeping them in. I stood at the front of the line, at the end of the line, in the middle. Nothing worked.

52

"What helped? It improved when they got to know me as a person. They responded to me after I played ball with them, after I took one of the kids to buy a pair of sneakers on 125th Street, after I broke up a couple of fights."

Mr. M. had sufficient resources to overcome the shock of these initial encounters with the class and to look at the causes of his difficulty. He saw that his lack of knowledge and his inexperience contributed to the trouble he was having. He began to make changes. He described what happened in these words:

"I didn't have the routines set in my mind. I had even forgotten how to say the pledge to the flag. Every kind of movement was rough. I didn't know how to get the kids to hang up their coats. Distributing books was a problem. I had to work on getting the routines set in my mind.

"What helped was becoming more myself. I didn't lose the structure, but the way I gave directions changed. I stopped playing the sergeant. I became more natural and yet the structure was there.

"There was a period in which they tested me out. One day about five of them broke their pencil points and they started to go to the pencil sharpener one at a time. This was putting it up in front of me. I just casually walked over to one of them at the sharpener and took his pencil, not even stopping my talking as I did it. I had been told about being tested, so I didn't blow my cork.

"Another day one of the boys came over to talk to me with his hat on. I told him I wouldn't talk to him with his hat on. He got his back up and walked away. I didn't get excited. He came back later without his hat on."

Mr. M. sought curriculum approaches which would allow him to maintain effective control of the class and at the same time interest the children. "A trouble spot for me was handling transitions from one subject to the other. At first what I tried to do was give a brief introduction to the importance of the subject we were going to study. After a while I discovered a better way: to have each lesson grow out of the one before. For example, we'd move from a study of the prices of things in the stores to looking at transportation and how food came to New York from other parts of the country and the world.

"One of the hardest things was to have the children see the relationship between school and what happens in their own lives. I was forever on the lookout for opportunities to do this. For example, when someone talked about a policeman pushing someone around, I used this to move into a discussion of how they think a policeman feels working in the neighborhood. We went on to find out about civil service, about how someone gets to be a policeman, the preparation he needs, the salary he gets. When they began to see the whole scope of what it takes to be a policeman, it was a small start on changing their attitudes toward the cop on the corner."

Mr. M. recalled that the school day was not entirely made up of dismal moments. "Some good things happened, too. Every day for about three weeks, two or three representatives of the class would come over to me to ask if I'd be coming back the next day. I told them I'd be their teacher until June, and that made a big difference.

"They began to respond to my routines. In fact, they thrived on them. They were happy to have someone check their work and hang their papers around the room. I put up a homework chart, and from only two or three doing their homework it jumped to everyone doing his work. Their eagerness helped me.

"I guess another important thing was that I genuinely liked them. I thought they were real kids. I enjoyed talking to them."

Mr. M. learned, in time, something of the complexity of the art of teaching, of the need to mesh one's individual personality with the needs of a particular group of children.

"The children accepted me as a person long before they got to know me as a teacher. I'd have some of them come up to the room during the lunch hour. After an informal lunch hour I'd still have discipline trouble in the afternoon. I tried to get a formal classroom situation going and I couldn't. The kids needed a consistent picture of me in order to respond consistently. I was much more comfortable being informal. But my picture of a teacher was someone in a jacket and tie sitting aloof and cold behind a desk. That wasn't my style. I had to develop new concepts of teaching. I told myself at first that I wasn't teaching. All I was doing was guidance, social work, disciplining. I didn't realize that you can't do any teaching unless the children relate to you and you relate to them. I had to learn more about what I felt about myself, about what I believe, about who I am. I had to learn what I really felt about children who came from backgrounds that were strange to me.

"I became more aware and less defensive in time as I learned about the neighborhood and the children. I remember that I went to a neighborhood church one Sunday. Seeing the kids that way was different. It made them look at me differently."

The first year for Mr. M. was a year filled with significant events. Certain occurrences and ideas stood out clearly in his mind.

"What I remember most of that first year was the real personal contacts I made. I remember where each child sat, even his name. One boy made a remark that, I guess, is significant. He said, 'This must be your first year of teaching. Nobody spent as much time with us before.'

"Another thing I remember is the assistant principal reminding me that even if I was successful in some of the things that I did, that I oughtn't to rest, that I had to keep trying new things. This idea still keeps me interested, keeps me thinking."

One incident will, in all likelihood, remain in Mr. M.'s memory throughout his professional career. It was an encounter with a troubled, thirteen-year-old boy whom we will call James. Mr. M. recalled this event: "The one thing I'll never forget was rolling on the floor with James. You came along and got me out of it by grabbing him. I went home that afternoon muttering to myself. I knew I could never let that happen again. I had lost my temper and I had put him on the plane of another adult, or, you might say, I came down to the level of a child. As a matter of fact, I wasn't that annoyed at James. I was annoyed at the class and it was close to three o'clock. I had had it with the class and I took it out on James. Now I can handle things differently. I know when I'm on guard, when I'm irritated."

Mr. M. eventually succeeded in developing the feeling of a class with a group of children who had lost almost all sense of class morale. He succeeded because he thought about what happened, he applied himself with energy, and he showed a determination to work out the problems that arose. He was helped by his previous experience with the children and the school through his sister and through his college work. In addition, once in the classroom his personal resources were given support and free rein to operate.

For example, the incident with James described above could have been totally destructive. Instead it became the basis for self-examination, for an interchange of ideas, and for eventual learning. The day after it occurred Mr. M. apologized for what happened. He was assured that it was understandable how a day of frustration could lead to a loss of control. The events that led up to the incident were examined. James had been playing with some coins. Mr. M. took them, and James attempted to get them back. The wild battle ensued. The importance of personal property to ghetto children was thus violently illustrated. When the teacher has built up a feeling of trust between himself and the child, he can then, with little trouble, ask to hold distracting material until the end of the day.

The daily conferences held with the assistant principal during the beginning period served as a sounding board for the teacher, as a means of support, and as an aid in helping him evaluate and deal with his problems. Mr. M. emphasized the cathartic value offered by "bull sessions." The daily conferences, and talks with his sister and with his friends, all helped him to stick with what was often a wearing situation.

At the daily conferences books were evaluated, plans were reviewed, audio-visual materials were made available, teaching ideas were suggested, and the respective roles of the supervisor and teacher were considered. For example, it was decided that particularly at the outset the assistant principal would remain out of the classroom and allow Mr. M. to cultivate the allegiance of the class. This was deemed necessary because for the previous month the class had been accustomed to taking their problems to the assistant principal.

In class the children filled out time budgets, and these revealed that viewing television and participating in athletics were the two activities in which the most time was spent. Some of the boys were greatly interested in physical culture and devoted hours to exercises. Others were interested in listening to records. Almost all of them had to spend time doing household chores.

This information was used as a guide to curriculum planning. For example, the children were given the opportunity to talk about their hobbies. The interest in sports was utilized for writing letters to favorite sports heroes, for planning a class field day, and for learning game techniques and procedures. A discussion of household chores led to a study of how to shop, how to care for money, and ways to earn money.

Ideas came from experienced teachers as they joined the informal lunch-hour discussions. One teacher indicated how playing soft music as the children entered the room helped to create a relaxed atmosphere. Another illustrated how he always tried to maintain the appearance of class control by, in some cases, giving assent to a violation of class rules. For example, the teacher can tell a child who refuses to take his seat when requested to do so that it is all right to stand until he is ready to work. This may help to avoid a situation of open defiance. Another teacher pointed to the need not only to correct deviant practices but to provide instruction in acceptable procedures.

Thus these first months were months in which learning occurred despite many stress-filled moments. Learning resulted because previous experience, positive attitudes, and an open intelligence combined with an atmosphere of support and clear channels of communication to create a situation where problems were expressed, evaluated, and treated.

From this view of the experiences of a new teacher, it may be helpful to see how the children in a ghetto elementary school perceive their teachers and the ways in which they feel their teachers affect how they learn.

4 What do the children have to say?

The children in the ghetto enter their classrooms for the first time, eyes focused like biologists examining a strange organism under a microscope, waiting for movement, waiting for clues to the character of the person under examination. They silently ask the questions that possibly all children in all classes ask, but they await the answers with more fearful anticipation.

"Will he be strict?"

"Can I do exactly as I want?"

"Does he mean what he says?"

"Will he think I'm stupid?"

"Will he like me?"

The children find the replies to their questions quickly, because they possess to a high degree the ability to move to the core of the teacher's personality and make accurate judgments. They have definite ideas about the kind of teacher who helps them learn. In describing this kind of teacher they gave the following ideas:

"A teacher who helps you to learn is in between, a little on the strict side, a little on the kind-hearted side."

"A strict teacher holds you down; a simple teacher lets you do what you want."

"She laid the laws down; she told us what we could do and what we couldn't do."

"A teacher has to be understanding and press you more."

"He should be mean and nice."

"He means what he says."

"A good teacher shows that he has a like for the children."

When asked to elaborate on what was meant by such words as "strict," the children gave some of the following examples:

"The children knew what the teacher would do if they didn't behave. She'd call for their mother if she had to."

"When she told the children she was going to do something, she'd do it."

"She doesn't let people walk around, get water any time they want."

"She doesn't call on the principal every five minutes for help. She takes care of her own."

"He stands up for his rights as a teacher. He doesn't let the children run over him. I think sometimes teachers are a-scared of the children. They think that maybe if they come along and take a boy's comic book, he'll pick up a chair and hit the teacher. They read stories of things like people getting stabbed and they're scared. I think if the teacher wouldn't be scared, the children wouldn't have the nerve to touch the teacher."

"She doesn't yell all the time. If she yells, the children will yell. If she talks it all out slowly, you'll understand it more."

In describing other aspects of the approach of teachers who helped them to behave and to learn, children made these comments:

60

What do the children have to say?

"She thinks we're young gentlemen and ladies."

"She tells us we're better than kids who are always running around. Other teachers won't say anything about kids cursing or running around."

"She makes clear to us if we don't hear what's said it'll be hard on us. We won't pass tests."

"When someone's disturbing the class, she don't mention names. She'll say, 'Someone's holding us back.' This is good because other children be talking too."

"The teacher explains what the boy or girl did, and that helps."

The children were in almost total agreement about certain positive qualities of teachers. One such quality is described by a boy who said: "My teacher always takes time with you. Even though we have a big class, if a child doesn't know she takes time to make sure he understands. I think if we had teachers who took more time, we'd have a better school."

In response to the question about how teachers helped them learn, child after child gave replies similar to the following:

"He gives time after school."

"He takes more time with you."

"The teacher gives you time after school to talk about your problems."

"If some child is having it hard in math, the teacher keeps him in and helps. This helps the kid and kind of makes the teacher feel better."

. On the other hand, the kind of teacher who made learning harder was the one who didn't want to give time to explain. One child put it this way: "Some teachers don't have patience. They put a certain tone in their voice, an angry tone. You get nervous and you think you're not catching on quick enough. Maybe, you think, you should be in a dumber class."

Another child commented: "I get mad when the teacher just marks the example wrong. A teacher who is understanding explains the mistakes to you, asks you why you left out part of the example."

A third child said, "I can't learn if the teacher gets mad when you don't understand."

Why this pressing desire for a teacher who takes time, who has patience, who "puts things on the board and explains things clearly," who "teaches easy parts first, step by step," who "if you don't know something and you get mad will come over and help you to learn," and "who makes sure you understand"? It may be that a child has been called stupid too often before, has begun to believe in the truth of the label, and is defensive about any situation that lends substantiation to the charge. It may be that too frequently the child's needs have been ignored, and anything but immediate attention recalls feelings of rejection. The remarks of the children give evidence of this reaction:

"I get mad when the teacher asks me to wait when I need help. He may be helping someone else, but still I get mad."

"When the teacher sits at the desk and I can't see the board, I get mad."

It may be that certain children move with the slower style described by Frank Riesmann in *The Culturally Deprived Child,* and are rattled by teachers who insist on speedy responses. The following statements point to this idea:

"When the teacher goes too fast, I can't learn."

"If the teacher gives too much work at once, I get mad."

"I get messed up on division because it takes a long time to do."

"A kind teacher has patience when you try to figure out an answer."

"Some teachers don't give children time enough to understand."

Almost all of the children expressed the idea that a teacher who gave them homework helped them to learn. In respectful tones they told of teachers who gave them a lot of homework or who gave them homework every day. The teacher who was work-oriented was the teacher who, in the view of the children, helped them learn. The children's statements are revealing of this idea:

"She puts work on the board and you do it."

"She gives us study sheets."

"The teacher gave us a lot of words to learn."

"She prepared us for reading tests by giving us vocabulary expansion papers."

"When children come to our class because their class is split up, the teacher gives them work also."

"She helped us remember the planets by teaching us a poem."

"The teacher gave me books to read, and he helped me with some of the things I didn't know."

"The teacher checks your work."

Children appreciated teachers who gave praise when it was due:

"She congratulates with a speech when you do something good."

"She gave people stars that do nice."

"She says we're better than kids that run around."

Children also indicated that when teachers were concerned with the feelings of the students, it helped them learn. For example, one child remarked: "The teacher understands that children may have trouble, and when she asks what's the matter, you can tell her and feel a little better."

Another child said: "She knows how we feel inside. She lets us write about how we feel. She tells us she feels the same things sometimes."

The way teachers presented material affected how children felt about the way they learned. These methods were described as follows:

"She doesn't give us the answers. She doesn't tell us if it's wrong or not. She asks the class if they think it's wrong or not. You've got to speak up if you think it's right."

"It's like a game the way she teaches the multiplication facts. She gets the bead board and asks you your ideas about it. She writes it on the blackboard and asks you to come up and work it out. She takes time to make sure you understand. She goes over it again and again."

Children felt teachers also helped them learn by taking them on trips, punishing them when they did something wrong, telling jokes, and playing with them. They also thought it important that the teacher not always remain sitting behind his desk. When the children were asked what things teachers did that made it harder for them to learn, they spoke of things that made them angry, confused, and upset. Teachers who scream were pointed to immediately as teachers who made learning harder. One child described her reaction this way: "All the yelling and stuff, it seem like your brain it get all mixed up when she be hollering and screaming."

Other children said the following:

"Yelling doesn't help. Every time the teacher yelled people got more mad."

"He kept yelling at me. I didn't understand the work when he kept yelling. I just didn't do it."

"When the teacher yells at me, I get nervous and scared. I get afraid the teacher's going to hurt me."

"When the teacher yells, she forgets what she's doing and goes on to something else."

"The yelling teacher upsets the whole class."

In the children's view, other teachers contribute to learning difficulty through the use of sudden, loud noises. For example, one child said: "The teacher banged on his desk with his ruler. It got me nervous. It made me jump."

Other children gave similar reactions:

"I don't like it when the teacher slams the door. It hurts my ear. It makes it harder to learn."

What do the children have to say?

"When the teacher slams the door, I forget what I was thinking about."

"The teacher used to ring a cowbell loud. After a while nobody hardly paid any attention to it. It was just another loud noise."

When teachers isolated children in the hall outside the room, the children felt this had a bad effect on them. One child gave the feeling of many when he said, "When the teacher throws you out of the room, out in the hallway, you feel like a fool and lonely because everybody else is studying."

Other children stated their feelings as follows:

"I feel when out of the room like she won't let me come back any more, like the teacher don't want you."

"I feel so ashamed in the hallway. You feel like people are looking at you and laughing at you."

"I feel stupid out in the hallway. You don't learn anything out of the room."

Of course, there are occasions when children need to be removed from a situation. Often the manner in which this takes place is of prime importance. Some schools and teachers send a child to another room to calm down and allow him to return when he feels ready. When such a removal is handled calmly, the child can appreciate it as helping him to gain control of himself, rather than as a sign of rejection by the teacher.

Teachers who use physical force are not unknown to the children, as revealed by their statements:

"When the teacher hits you, you don't want to do your work. You do the same thing over again."

"Some teachers hit you and never explain why."

"Teachers make you nervous by hitting on you. I get scared the teacher will keep hitting on you for doing nothing."

"The teacher hitting on you makes you mad, and you want to punish the teacher for punishing you."

A small group of children felt teachers were justified in hitting children. Their remarks indicate that they may reflect the values expressed by their parents.

"My father said if the teacher hits you, he must have a good reason."

"If the children don't have respect for the teacher, the teacher should hit them."

"A teacher's gotta hit you sometime."

Teachers who call children names caused disordered classroom situations in some cases. Some of the children had the following negative reactions:

"Some teachers call the children stupid. They call them crazy and dumb. Then the children act that way to get even with the teacher."

"The teacher calls a child an idiot, and he gets mad when the child calls the teacher an idiot back."

"Calling children names makes children feel bad. They get mad, and then the smaller children see the bigger children doing things that are bad and they copy them."

"The teacher who is sarcastic makes it harder to learn."

It is clear from the children's remarks that many of them are extremely fearful of being physically hurt, of being rejected, and of being regarded as incompetent. This is further evidenced by children who visibly flinch at the approach of an authority figure with whom they are not familiar; by children who interpret the absence of their regular teacher as proof that she doesn't care about them; and by children who, in a rage, "ball up" their papers when the teacher has marked an example wrong.

When children were asked what advice they would give to a teacher coming to their school, they gave further indication of this need for reassurance, acceptance, and a feeling of safety:

"Be friendly with the children and they'll be friendly with you. You'll get along and they'll do their lessons and their homework and they'll learn."

What do the children have to say?

"You should be nice with the children, and they'll be nice with you. The children will get used to you."

"The teacher should understand that all children are not children who won't listen to their teachers."

"You have to be strict on the kids. They're not bad. Try not to let the children have their own way or they'll run over you."

"The teacher should make everybody do the work. She shouldn't play favorites by always sending the same child on errands. Some teachers think only about one person."

"Don't ignore children. The teacher shouldn't turn away when the child asks a question."

"You could fuss at children a little bit, but just don't hit."

All of these comments indicate some of the qualities of depressed-area elementary schoolchildren. Teachers' observations, classroom questionnaires filled out in connection with other school projects, and interviews conducted with children all point out other unique characteristics. Teachers repeatedly remarked on the strength and resiliency of the children. They made such comments as the following:

"You have a strong child who, when he is exposed to the experiences our children have had, can come to school and still learn."

"They've had to endure so much more than other children. The strength is there."

"They don't quit. Even though they've had a devil of a time trying to learn to read, they're still willing to try if the teacher tries it another way."

The interviews showed that the children are apparently reluctant to participate orally on an individual basis. A group situation allowed children to verbalize their ideas more freely. The child who was reticent in an individual interview often became an active contributor in the group interview. It may have been that, in addition to the company provided by his peers, the child was given time to think as others presented ideas, and thus he did not feel the pressure of an expected immediate response.

Children in the ghetto have a unique experience with responsibility. It is not uncommon for a ten-year-old child to be given the duty of caring for the needs of younger siblings and of managing household chores. This sense of responsibility does not necessarily carry over to the school. Rather, many teachers noted that for many children unpleasant home responsibility results in a desire to avoid responsibilities in school. Moreover, the abruptness with which some children must assume responsibility deprives them of the delights and satisfaction of being cared for as babies. This longing for a return to that brief period of infantilism is evidenced by the number of children who even in the upper grades seek the oral satisfaction of thumb-sucking. (A survey conducted with the teachers of the fourth, fifth, and sixth grades in one Harlem elementary school revealed that twenty out of 425 children, an average of one or two in each class, continued to regress to thumb-sucking.)

Despite this early need for ghetto children to become involved in the daily struggle for existence, they do develop perspective enough to be fully aware of the conditions in which they live and to express a desire for change. Any thought that elementary schoolchildren in the ghetto are apathetic about their status is belied by an informal questionnaire filled out by sixty sixth-grade children. In answer to a question about where they would like to live, only five of the sixty indicated that they wanted to live where they now resided. Of the sixty children queried about things they would like to see changed in their neighborhood, only four failed to include some item, and even these four blank responses may have been due to reasons other than not desiring some kind of change.

There was a pattern to the changes the children felt were needed. They included repairing houses in poor condition, build-

ing better places for people to live, constructing two-floor buildings, erecting projects to take the place of old buildings, having
cleaner streets, stopping people from throwing litter in the
streets, cleaning rubbish from empty lots, cleaning dirty air-
shafts, building more parks and playgrounds, providing more
play streets and recreation centers, getting the "junkies" out of
the neighborhood, placing drug addicts in jail, having all the
"bad people" move, getting people to stop drinking and stealing,
and having more men teachers in school.

Another questionnaire was filled out by 120 children in a
Harlem elementary school. This was part of a plan to evaluate
changes in their attitudes which might occur as a result of a
sharing of activities and visits with a school in a white middle-
class neighborhood. An analysis of this questionnaire revealed
other characteristics of Negro elementary schoolchildren. It
indicated that, although many of the children thought they were
equal in most ways to white children, they believed the white
children perceived them as more likely to fight, as learning less
in their schools, as being less interested in school, and as being
less intelligent than white children. This was consistent with the
thought of most of the Negro children that the white children
would not want to go to school with them. Surely there are values
to be gained by an exchange of visits between classes of Negro
children and classes of white children, but the visits must be
carefully planned if the values are to be realized.

A description of one incident may shed some light on the
values which may result from such an interchange. During the
course of a visit of white children to the class and school of
Negro children, two of the visitors almost got into a fight. Two
of the Negro children reported this occurrence to the assistant
principal, great glee showing on their faces. It was almost as if
they were saying, "Look, we're not so bad, so wild after all.
Other children have fights, too."

A handbook for teaching in the ghetto school

The comments of the children, their reactions to questionnaires, and their behavior patterns as observed by teachers indicate that many ghetto children are affected by the tumult and chaos of their environment. Many of them react negatively in school to anything which implies rejection, physical punishment, or denigration. But they eagerly seek the approval of those teachers who initiate and maintain structure, who display patience, who develop a work atmosphere, who give praise, and who show concern for their feelings. In addition, many of them show a remarkable resiliency and an ability to seek change and maintain a faith in the possibility that change can occur.

5 What can I teach?

The new teacher in a ghetto elementary school is confronted by a complex interplay of forces. In the classroom, for example, there is an exchange of feelings and experiences between the teacher and children. Their respective strengths and weaknesses affect each other. Within the school the education of the children is modified by the kind of school plant that exists, the policy of the administration, the behavior of other teachers and children, and the curriculum requirements set down by the local board of education. The new teacher is also affected by the quality of parent involvement, by the demands of civil rights groups, by the values of the community, by the work of community agencies, and by the social and economic problems that exist.

A teacher who is aware of these forces, who understands them, and who is able to utilize them is more likely to develop

A handbook for teaching in the ghetto school

a curriculum that makes contact with the children. The following pages illustrate how teachers have made use of their knowledge of the children in an East Harlem elementary school to organize a meaningful curriculum.

MAKING USE OF A KNOWLEDGE OF CHILDREN'S EXPERIENCES

Successful teachers in the ghetto have used a knowledge of the past experiences of children to guide them as they help pupils to acquire new skills, new knowledge, and new attitudes. They know that the past experiences of children are their frame of reference for meeting new situations. Concepts and generalizations developed from previous experience guide the children's thinking and acting as they meet new situations and have new experiences. These teachers have tried to help the children discover the relationships that exist between their past experiences and present classroom activities.

Many children in ghetto elementary schools know southern agricultural life. A fifth-grade teacher described how he used this knowledge in dealing with an area of social studies:

> I was groping for a way to bring some reality to our class study of pioneer life when I discovered there were two boys in the class who had just come to New York from a farming area in South Carolina. I found out that I had other children who were also recent arrivals from the South. Many of the kids returned to the South for the summer vacations. Almost everyone in the class had some contact with southern farm life through relatives or friends.
>
> When a discussion arose about the pioneers getting buckets of water from a well, they knew what we were talking about. Double-decked beds in a one-room cabin was a concept very real to them. They knew what it meant to rough it in an undeveloped wilderness. I discussed hunting as it related to the pioneers, and I was talking to children who had gone possum hunting themselves. I could even talk about rotation of crops and it was something with which

they were directly familiar. They knew about crowded conditions, preservation of life, and adaptability to difficult surroundings better than any middle-class kid would. They knew it from their lives up here in New York and in the South.

During the course of our study of pioneer life I made a point of having the children tell about life on a southern farm. I asked them to describe such aspects of southern rural living as what they did about water and electricity, how they cared for animals, and how chores were divided. Those who had had these experiences enjoyed talking about them, because it gave them a sense of uniqueness in having seen and done things about which other children knew very little. We saw that sharing jobs was something we do here as well as in the South. We discussed how people in both North and South have to find ways of providing their own entertainment. We talked about the need to care for clothing and hard-to-replace household materials.

When we had these discussions, when I had them look at television programs about pioneers, when they read books about them, and when they viewed filmstrips about the early settlers, I think they did so with real interest, because in a way they were dealing with their own lives.

Other links to children's experiences are inherent in a study of pioneer life. There is a high rate of pupil movement into and out of slum communities. The question, "What caused your family to move to this neighborhood?" can be compared to the pioneer movement westward. Meaningful generalizations can be derived, such as:

People move for many reasons.

People worry about getting along well in a new place with little money.

People can make their surroundings attractive even in difficult times.

The subject of common illnesses and remedies which prevailed in pioneer times can ring a note of familiarity for children who know rural life. The children can learn about the possible damage that may result from insect or snake bites. They can find out about the sicknesses that beset farm animals. They can compare the manner in which illnesses and injuries are cared for in New York and in the South today with how they were cared for in pioneer days. They can determine likely causes of injury of pioneers by referring to their own experiences in country areas.

The relationship between the crafts used by pioneers and those used by a southern rural population can be examined. The children can learn about weaving, knitting, and constructing utensils of clay.

Thus the teacher who becomes acquainted with what the children know about rural life can plan activities which relate to and extend this knowledge.

Many children in the ghetto are responsible for spending a share of the family food budget. With working mothers leaving early in the morning, children are given relatively small sums with which to buy supper for the family. Money, therefore, becomes a matter of prime concern for these children. Food, too, achieves a position of great importance. This is borne out by the oft-repeated question of the child who, as his class discusses a forthcoming trip, asks, "Will there be food there?" Children with these thoughts and responsibilities can be helped to learn about nutrition and what constitutes a balanced diet, to discover the value of comparative shopping, to appreciate wise money management, and to become skilled in the use of money.

There are many possible experiences which will have value for the children. They can make personal budgets. They can compare food ads to determine best buys. They can survey stores for various prices. They can make a study of items that are taxed. They can learn about using newspaper advertisements for shopping. They can be helped to analyze critically their shopping experiences and the foods they eat. For example, one teacher reported how she helped children develop better dietary habits:

I noticed that a lot of our children eat sour pickles and a bag of potato chips for lunch. Others buy a sandwich made up of a roll and a single slice of meat. I saw something that needed teaching. We started to learn about good nutrition. We checked books. We interviewed the nurse about the value of different foods. We sent away to insurance companies for literature on nutrition. We evaluated the school lunches in terms of what makes a good diet. By referring to the nutritive value of foods, I tried to discourage the children from gobbling sour pickles, potato chips, or soda for lunch or for breakfast.

We also went on to find out the price of a roll in a bakery and figured what a slice of ham would cost using the price of a pound as our basis. The children saw that the price they were charged was way out of line.

Another teacher described how she helped her children become more intelligent consumers. Her class maintained a fund and shopped for material to decorate the room, for party refreshments, and for cleaning supplies. The children collected the money and kept an account book. They looked for sales, noted the advantage of buying in bulk, chose materials with a view toward quality and price, and evaluated their purchases. They became more aware of the various kinds of stores in the community as they visited pet shops to buy turtles and florist shops to buy plants and terrarium material.

Using the children's experiences with money management, the teacher can thus help to develop their skills in mathematics and extend their understanding of the social application of money.

Many children in slum areas have been exposed to undesirable experiences, such as living in extremely crowded conditions where responsibility can become overwhelming and comfort difficult. For example, one teacher in describing his group of children said, "They have gone through more by the time they get to school in the morning than middle-class children go through in a lifetime." He might have been referring to a child who wakes up bleary-eyed because his younger brother with whom he shares a bed has been coughing through the night.

Getting ready for school may consist of a ten-year-old child preparing breakfast for three or four younger siblings and getting them dressed as well. It may include sewing on a stray button, or ironing a shirt washed the previous night, or running an errand for a sleepy parent, or finding books that have been played with by a younger child and then temporarily misplaced. For some children, brushing teeth, washing, and breakfast are fitted in if time allows.

Children will be more likely to discuss their difficulties if the teacher neither deplores nor indicates how sorry he is about the situation. The children seek neither criticism nor sympathy, only acceptance. Teachers have described how, when these experiences have been brought out in the open, they are able to turn them into worthwhile educational content.

In one classroom a discussion of crowded living conditions resulted in positive learning. The teacher was able to get the children to talk about this problem by introducing his own difficulties in living in a small area. He described his small two-room apartment and the need for more room as his family became larger. He told about his lack of comfort living in close quarters and his hard search for another apartment. He was able to discuss with the children in a realistic way the need for thoughtfulness within a family, the need to take baths frequently when you're sharing a bed with one or two other children, the particular need to get home on time for meals when there are a lot of people to be fed, and the need for each person to do his share of the housework.

Children talked about how to keep personal belongings away from the curious hands of younger children and how to arrange an equitable sharing of the television set. It was suggested that children can get together with their brothers and sisters to organize corners which would be theirs and theirs alone. They made up time budgets in order to plan sensibly for the many home and school tasks. They also talked about how to make their living quarters cleaner and more attractive. They went into the need for being alone at times, and listed such places as the library and the park where it was possible to gain a measure of privacy.

Ghetto elementary schoolchildren also know about narcotics addicts. As early as age seven they are aware that narcotics addicts exist in their neighborhood. Children refer to particular blocks as "that bad block" when they know that addicts abound there. Some children are able to describe the procedures involved in taking narcotics because they have witnessed such acts. When children are asked what they would like to see changed in their neighborhood, they invariably refer to the need for getting rid of the addicts. Here, too, the teacher who doesn't moralize or express shock will probably find that the children will talk about what they have seen and what they know.

Although cases of addiction in the elementary school are rare, questions arise on the subject from the older children in particular. The teacher can present factual information regarding the effect of narcotics on general health and social behavior, the ways in which people are introduced to habit-forming drugs, and the relationship between addiction and crime. For most teachers it may seem somewhat premature to delve deeply into the problems of narcotics addiction. But the children are very much aware that the problem exists and do have questions, so the teacher should be prepared to provide information. (A possible background source for the teacher is the New York City Board of Education bulletin, *What Secondary Schools Can Do About Teenage Narcotics Addiction* [1956-57 Series No. 3].)

In a sixth-grade class the teacher used the question of cigarette smoking to arouse interest in the human body. One child had been reported for cigarette smoking outside of school. The teacher did not respond with a sermon. Rather, he indicated he was aware that others had tried cigarette smoking. He brought himself into the discussion by pointing out that the research on the causes of cancer had made him decide to stop smoking. He discussed with the class the effects of cigarette smoking on the human body. This led to an investigation of material that described how the human body operates. The children learned about the functions of various body organs. Questions arose about epilepsy, appendicitis, heart disease, diabetes, and other malfunctions with which the children were familiar. There was deep interest as the children discussed the symptoms and causes of diseases many of them had had.

A classroom situation *can* be created in which children will speak about the realities of their lives—including unpleasant experiences. The teacher who accepts these reports without shock can find the opportunity to use them with positive results.

MAKING USE OF A KNOWLEDGE OF CHILDREN'S INTERESTS

The deep, lasting interests of children can guide the teacher in approaching and choosing the curriculum. For example, many children in ghetto elementary schools are interested in learning about ways to earn money. One sixth-grade boy who worked for a full month doing errands, helping to clean the corner grocery store, carrying packages from a supermarket, and working at other sundry tasks, was stunned to discover that his month's savings of $18 was just enough to buy himself the coat he wanted so badly.

Children who are constantly on the alert for ways to make money, who seek out opportunities to make themselves useful so that they can obtain funds for themselves, and who have an intimate knowledge of the connection of money to well-being are quickly involved in class discussions of how to earn money. Teachers have used this interest to introduce children to the classified section of the newspaper. In this way children begin to become aware of the qualifications needed for certain jobs. They begin to see the "use value" of education.

Some teachers have sought means of giving children firsthand experience with the work people do. One teacher made a practice of bringing friends to class who told about their jobs and the skills needed for their positions. Visitors to school assemblies from the Civil Service Brigade and the Police and Fire Departments have told children how they got their jobs and what kind of educational background was required. Teachers describing how they obtained their jobs have brought a vivid sense of reality to the need for education. One teacher worked with a group of parents on how to take civil service tests and found this was a way of bringing the class discussion on jobs directly into the homes of the children. Children who have had day-to-day contact with such small-business enterprises as the corner grocery store and candy store have learned how individuals brought these stores into being. Children have discussed such jobs as elevator operator and street cleaner that are being outdated by automation. In some classes the vocational aspirations of children were listed and the educational prerequisites for goals were discussed.

Instruction which stresses the relationship between education and career advancement is necessary because children frequently reveal an almost total lack of awareness of the quality and degree of education needed for certain jobs. That this is a prevailing difficulty for low socioeconomic area children is given some substantiation by Kenneth Morland's study, which found significantly lower educational aspirations among lower-class children but no significantly different occupational aspirations. By placing a greater emphasis on occupational information, teachers can make use of an abiding interest and fill a real need for the children.

Many children in ghetto elementary schools are interested in the lives of people. Teachers report an inability to teach historical concepts with abstract facts as a base. For example, the statement "America was founded as a colony by England" is meaningless for most children because it presupposes a knowledge of what a colony is and where England is located. The children respond more readily when history is taught with the lives of people as a focus.

Identification with an explorer like Columbus is realized when teacher and children wonder together what is going to happen and what will be found. There can be vitality and excitement to a discussion of danger, escape from danger, the onslaught of a storm at sea, and the restless anger of troubled sailors.

Present-day events become more meaningful when they are dealt with in terms of people. Empathy with unemployed Appalachian miners is easily aroused in children who know firsthand the plight of men without work. Children can discuss such questions as: "Why do people lose their jobs?" "What can people do to get new jobs?" "How do people get along without jobs?" "What are the feelings of people out of work?"

Children can become involved in the reality of world happenings when such events as space exploration, Olympic trials, hurricane devastation, and the wartime havoc in Vietnam are discussed in terms of people. They respond to such questions as: "How do you think the astronauts feel before their flights into space?" "What kind of training do Olympic athletes undergo?" "What happens to people caught in the path of a hurricane?" "How are people affected by the fighting in Vietnam?"

Biographical material on the lives of such men as Joe Louis, Frederick Douglass, Magellan, and Columbus interests children because it offers insight into the lives of people who, through their own efforts, overcame obstacles. Children can relate their own childhood difficulties to the boyhood problems of these famous men. Success stories feed the hopes for a better life about which there is so much talk and thought.

Children enjoy the tall tales which tell of the feats of such legendary heroes as Paul Bunyan, John Henry, and Casey Jones. Through these stories they become more aware of the quality of the men who after a day of felling mighty trees sat around a campfire exchanging descriptions of the fabulous Paul and his blue ox. Stories about John Henry help them to see more clearly the struggles of men to push railroad construction to the farthest corners of the country. As they read these legends, as they write legends of their own, as they listen to folk song records which tell of legendary heroes, they can give vent to their natural inclination to dream and they can see the beauty and power in these dreams.

Children are fascinated by material that describes how people's lives are changing. They are taken by stories that tell about going to an integrated school, moving to a housing project, or traveling to a strange land. For example, a group of sixth-graders found *Mary Jane* by Dorothy Sterling extremely interesting because they knew about the term integration and could easily put themselves in the place of a lone Negro child attending a white school.

MAKING USE OF A KNOWLEDGE OF THE COMMON ACADEMIC DEFICIENCIES OF THE CHILDREN

Many children are deficient in specific areas of academic ability. These gaps in knowledge are often a direct result of environmental factors and of the child's previous schooling. Teachers who achieve success with the children recognize these deficiencies and understand their causes. They have faith in their ability

81

to eliminate areas of weakness and plan activities to overcome them.

Many children in ghetto elementary schools reveal an inability to listen, and much of the research done with environmentally impoverished children confirms this as a major area of weakness. The reasons for this lack of development are becoming clearer. Martin Deutsch indicates that in lower-class homes there tends to be less dinnertime conversation, and meals are less likely to be regularly scheduled affairs. Deutsch concludes that the most impoverished area of activity for low socioeconomic-area children is that of language feedback in adult-child interactions.

Almost without exception, teachers in depressed-area schools realize the pertinency of the listening problem. The following teacher comments illustrate this awareness:

"For all the talking they do, they don't communicate because they don't listen to each other."

"The slower children, in particular, don't hear you."

"If you put on the radio, children begin to talk to each other."

A systematic, focused approach is necessary to deal with this problem. A child who grows up in a home which is a maelstrom of different sounds—of television, of other children, of the street, and of strangers—must first of all learn to eliminate sound from his consciousness or he can develop no inner life of his own. The school must help him to become aware again of particular sounds. To do this, it becomes necessary to arrange an environment with a minimum of extraneous distraction. Teachers who know this begin to control the stimuli within the classroom. Some go so far as to cover the window of the door to prevent the distraction of children in the hallway peering into the room. They limit the moving of furniture to certain periods. They use softly modulated voices. They carefully routinize such class activities as the sharpening of pencils and going to the lavatory.

82

Another cause of poor listening is that children have found their past schoolwork irrelevant to their experience. So the successful teacher seeks every means to heighten interest in classroom activity as a way of sharpening the quality of listening that occurs. Some teachers have accomplished this by personalizing discussions. For example, the teacher who initiates a discussion of weekend activity by asking children what they did is less likely to get the children to listen to each other closely than the teacher who begins by describing something he did over the weekend and telling what it meant to him.

Other teachers have used the children's interest in novelty and make-believe to obtain better listening. For example, they allow different children to assume the role of the teacher in giving spelling tests or in acting as leader in a class game. Teachers have found that children attend closely to dramatizations of such narrative poems as "The Creation" by James Weldon Johnson.

Some teachers have discovered that discussions with the children in an informal setting (sitting around a lunchroom table, standing together in the outside playground) helped to improve the quality of listening. They reported the amazement of the children that someone took the time to listen and to show interest. That this is something to which they are unaccustomed is evidenced by the blank, bewildered look in response to the question, "What do you talk about at home?"

In the informal discussions the teachers found that many children acted as though the only way to get someone to listen was to shout. The teachers had to assure them that they would get a chance to talk, and to remind them to listen to the person talking. The teachers, too, participated in these conversations. They reported that the children really opened up to each other, and that some talks lasted as long as an hour.

Teachers indicated many planned experiences designed to improve the listening ability of the children. Some of these were:

A handbook for teaching in the ghetto school

1. Listening to sounds in the classroom, sounds on a walk through the park, sounds of the street.

2. Retelling a story heard on the radio.

3. Identifying the source of sounds made by objects behind a screen.

4. Using the telephone to act out imaginary conversations.

5. Listening to records to pick out particular musical instruments.

6. Listening for words that rhyme.

7. Using the tape recorder to rehearse for assembly programs.

Teachers in ghetto elementary schools have found that many children in their classes have, in fact, learned *not* to listen. To counteract this they try to create an environment in which people listen courteously and attentively to each other. They do this by setting the appropriate example themselves, by introducing activities that command interest, by developing a calm, controlled atmosphere, and by concentrating on listening as a skill that needs to be taught.

Many of the children use language that is a distortion of standard English. Teachers often remark at their initial inability to understand children as they speak their parts during assembly programs. It is only with time that they become tuned in to the children's language.

It is not surprising that many children reveal a lack of subject continuity and syntactical organization when one considers that the language used in lower-class homes is generally limited and poorly structured. It is not astonishing that many children are reluctant to communicate individually when one sees how quickly they are made aware that their language is inept compared with the well-spoken teacher's. It is not strange that the children use their own unique slang as perhaps another way of displaying resistance to authority by rejecting the language represented by the school. It is possible, however, to show the children the speech patterns appropriate to particular situations.

One teacher reported a device for helping children become

more aware of their language habits. So that they could be motivated, he made up a "Slur Zoo" with the admonition "Don't let the *slurs* escape." Typical slurs were illustrated and placed on the bulletin board. Two examples of such slurs were:

"Didja?"

"Didja do your homework?"

"Betcha."

"Betcha I can run
faster than you!"

The children were taken by this graphic way of showing their speech habits. They began to look to their own speech and to the speech of their classmates for typical patterns and to make up illustrations of their own. In this way the children were helped to think more carefully about their speech and how it might be improved.

Another teacher told of using a dialect poem by Paul Laurence Dunbar. After interest in the poem had been firmly established, the reasons for distortion of language were discussed. The children enjoyed "translating" the poem into appropriate English. And because of the enjoyment they experienced in hearing the poem, they saw that dialect does have a role to play in literature.

Some teachers have sought out opportunities for children to use speech in situations which demand clear communication. They arranged for the children to read simple stories to younger children. They tape-recorded imaginary job interviews as a way of alerting the children to the value of good speech. They arranged for some children to use the school public address system to make school-wide announcements. Choral reading activities were used to help take away feelings of self-consciousness and to give the children positive reactions to their speech efforts.

Most of the teachers did not think it wise to imitate the slang of the children or adopt incorrect speech patterns as a means of gaining acceptance. They felt this may be interpreted as patronizing and is not appropriate to the teacher's leadership role.

The child who begins to see authority as an accepting figure rather than as a represser and sermonizer, who has many opportunities to express himself in an atmosphere of security, and who has occasion to hear models of good speech can develop a desire to improve his speech and to use language more correctly. Perhaps the most important factor in helping children express themselves more correctly is the teacher who can communicate his sincere interest in what the children have to say.

Many children in ghetto elementary schools read below their grade level. One child rapidly shakes his leg as he attempts to read to his teacher. Another child laboriously finger-points his way through a few pages of a basal reader and then slams it shut in utter frustration. Such children often rebel at the idea of attending an after-school session in remedial reading. These are children for whom reading means failure in school and failure in themselves. An approach to reading that results in distasteful labor, joyless exposure to unintelligible concepts, meaningless experience, and alienation from the teacher is neither practical nor sensible and perhaps is even cruel.

In *Teacher,* Sylvia Ashton-Warner gives a clue to an approach that can make contact with the children:

> Words and stories must have an intense meaning.
> Words and stories must be already part of the dynamic life.
> Words must be made of the stuff of the child himself, whatever and wherever the child.

What can I teach?

Teachers tell of children who come to the phrase "cup and saucer" in their readers, read the word "cup," but are stopped by the word "saucer." The word "elevator" stumps the child who has never seen an elevator. A child confronts the sentence "Billy sat on his porch"; he is able, with painful deliberation, to sound out the word "porch," but he doesn't know its meaning. Substitute the word "stoop" for "porch" and the sentence becomes clear. The word "cat" is the classical first word to enter a child's reading vocabulary. Yet a walk through the ghetto reveals few cats—as house pets they take money for feeding. On the other hand, the word "rat" takes little teaching. Children can describe the size of them, how their parents catch them, the sounds they make at night. When the teacher records the words and stories of the children which tell of real experiences, the child sees meaning, he sees teacher acceptance of his unpleasant reality without deprecation, and he sees the connection between the spoken and written word.

Books that are painfully white, non-urban, insipid in content, with pictures completely foreign to the children, will very likely produce mechanical, sterile reading. Some books do make contact. Teachers tell of books containing tales of fantasy, books on science fiction, books that describe the lives of far-off people which do interest the children, which do appeal to their very vivid imaginations. A teacher, referring to the ability of the children to relate to a world of fantasy, said, "They have to have vivid imaginations to get away from their everyday world of dreariness."

Fairy tales can permit the discussion of conflict situations which the children might ordinarily reject because of their proximity to reality. Florence Roswell and Gladys Natchez, in their book *Reading Disability,* give the example of *Boots and His Brothers* as a story especially satisfying to boys. In this story Boots is always the underdog—the child rejected by his brothers as well as his parents. He succeeds in performing a series of difficult tasks and conquers all obstacles in the end. Such resolution can be emotionally satisfying to children who have experienced similar feelings of rejection.

Those biographical tales which depict the lives of people who have risen above disaster are stories that reach the children, because they identify so strongly with those who have suffered misfortune. These stories often point to the need for perseverance in the face of failure. They show that it is possible to achieve success, love, respect, and fame even after one has been ridiculed and rejected and has experienced failure in school.

Books assume real meaning for the children when they are used to follow up classroom experiences. For example, one teacher reported how books on alligators and other animals attracted the children after he had brought a pet alligator into class.

Teachers have described methods which obviate the problem of teaching from books, if books are associated in the child's mind with failure. One teacher made summaries of stories she had read during the summer and had them copied for use by the children. Another took the developmental vocabulary contained in the basal reader and made up realistic stories using this vocabulary. Other teachers have used filmstrips as a source of reading material. One teacher utilized the opaque projector to flash on the board words of songs which the children read together. Another teacher made effective use of problems in mathematics to teach reading. The children saw the immediacy of solutions to problems, and so the reading brought with it immediate gratification. All of the teachers who were interviewed made use of experience charts that dealt with such matters as walks through the park, rides on a subway, and ways to improve the neighborhood.

Reading is a prevailing difficulty for many ghetto children. It needs the approach of a teacher who is inventive, who knows and accepts the children, who is acquainted with the kind of literature that will attract them, and who has a knowledge of the many techniques that must be used in the teaching of reading.

MAKING USE OF A KNOWLEDGE OF CHILDREN'S STRENGTHS

Most discussions of elementary schoolchildren in depressed areas dwell on their deficiencies. Almost no attention is given to the strengths they bring into the classroom. A teacher who recognizes these strengths can help to counteract the idea that a teacher in the ghetto is faced with intellectual and emotional cripples. The teacher can plan experiences which make use of the power that exists.

Many children in the ghetto display a knack for expressive language. A child who describes a hole in a sock as a "potato in the shoe" and a child who sees a cloud as "the color of ham fat" both reveal an ability to use expressive language. Children who can insult each other with a neat turn of phrase are not totally without language ability. This use of highly figurative language, understood only by the initiated, may be the children's way of showing their power over society and authority.

Teachers have created channels through which this language can flow. They have succeeded in giving the children the feeling that their hopes, their ideas, their wishes, and their plans are important, interesting, and realistic. Through an unjudging acceptance of children's reports of their experiences, and through an encouragement of an expression of dreams and wishes for change, teachers have stimulated children to write about such topics as "My Autobiography," "Things I Would Like to Change in My Neighborhood," "Life on Mars," and "My Dream House." Children can, in this way, give vent to their feelings of anger and to their desire for greater control over their environment. They begin to see that the language they use permits the enjoyable play of imagination, that there is an audience for stories of their past, and that there is acceptance of the idea of possible change.

Since the children's own language is filled with figurative speech, it is no surprise that they are fascinated by idioms. Teachers have reported lively class discussions of such idiomatic clichés as "a stone's throw away" or "his eyes are bigger than his stomach." They have helped children gain a better understanding of these idioms by having them draw illustrations of such sentences as "He had itchy fingers."

Teachers have made a game of the almost constant repartee of anger. After exposing children to many stories with dialogue, they suggest to children that they write their own dialogue stories on such topics as "A War of Words" or "Two Angry People."

Some teachers permit children to express their grievances in a written or oral manner. One teacher put up a complaint box to which the children contributed their gripes. These were read and discussed with the class. Other teachers reported how the children, in small groups, discussed things in school that helped them learn and things that prevented them from learning. The very fact that the teacher listened was a stimulus to further expression and a sign of respect for the worth of what the children had to say. As the children began to note a respect for their language efforts, they began to see its value and to develop a desire to utilize it more effectively and more grammatically.

Many of these children show great curiosity about living things, especially the pets a teacher brings to class. One class which had hamsters, white mice, and an alligator was beset by visitors from other classes who were eager to inspect the animals. This class, made up of the slowest group of children in the grade, moved without reluctance to books which told about the life and care of these animals.

The teacher can unlock this curiosity by being curious himself. Teachers tell of taking walks through the park and suddenly seeing shiny rocks. The rocks are studied, admired, collected, and read about. "Listen to the sound of crickets," one teacher says, her face alive with inquisitiveness, and the children hear a sound always around them in the park but never heard before.

Many of the children have never learned to look at things closely. This may be due to their never having had toys or objects to manipulate and study over a period of time, or it may be a result of the chaos of their environments, or it may be that they have never been taught to do so. Teachers have been able to use the children's curiosity to sharpen their perception. Children feel the fur of a rabbit brought into class. They look at its eyes, the way it walks, the manner in which it feeds. They see the shape of a blade of grass as a teacher points it out on a walk in the park. They feel its texture. They go to visit the neighborhood pet shop and perhaps for the first time they notice the animals there.

A teacher brought in a model of an eye, and the children followed with avid interest a discussion of the function of its various parts. When teachers have brought flowers from their gardens or shells from the shore, they have found that children move easily and enthusiastically into a study of these things. Setting up and caring for aquariums and terrariums have caused children to delve into books on the subject, to write up results, and to develop a sense of pride and possession in their room.

There are children in almost every intermediate grade who know from personal experience about raising pigeons. They can describe the care of pigeons, their habits, how they mate, and the illnesses they have. They can answer the questions of other children. They can investigate books to find the answers to their own questions about pigeon raising.

A teacher brought an incubator to class and the children were fascinated by the hatching of baby chicks. Children from other classes were tremendously eager to see this fantastic event.

Another teacher brought in a praying mantis cocoon. To see the thousands of tiny praying mantises emerge from the cocoon and, in an hour's time, change color was a cause of wonderment for both teacher and children.

Children's curiosity is put to daily use when they have an opportunity to grow their own plants in class. For a while the plants will be examined a few times a day for growth, and the first sign of vegetation will be a cause for joy. For a child who has not often had the privilege of owning objects, a plant of his own can be a treasured item.

The great need for the children to touch things can be met, at least in part, by the teacher who has in his room such things as insect exhibits, rock collections, terrariums, live pets, flower displays, and collections of shells. Class exploration of these things can lead to reading, writing, and discussion that is exciting and interesting for teachers and for children.

Effective use of children's curiosity calls for a classroom in which children are accustomed to asking questions. (An excellent, detailed description of such a classroom can be found in *More Than Social Studies* by Alice Miel and Peggy Brogan [pp. 148-180].)

MAKING USE OF A KNOWLEDGE OF CHILDREN'S FEELINGS

The feelings of children are a facet of all curriculum content. They affect children's reactions to the presentation of material. Children will not accept or become involved with curriculum content that does not take their feelings into account. When children sense that their vital needs—as represented by their inner emotions—are understood and dealt with, then communication and cooperation are encouraged.

Many children in the ghetto are afraid of change. The school attempts to bring some kind of order to their chaotic lives, but certain changes in day-to-day routine necessarily occur. For example, most of the sixth-grade children upon promotion attend the neighborhood junior high school. The prospect of this radical change, coupled with the tales the children hear in the streets, combine to bring on feelings of great trepidation. So traumatic are these feelings for some children that their parents try to place them in the supposedly more tranquil surroundings of other junior high schools.

One sixth-grade class was exposed to a typical orientation lesson on the forthcoming experience in the junior high school. The guidance counselor described the system of changing classes, the different subject teachers, the shops, the club program, and the honor societies. After she left the children commented: "That was a phony. It's not that way. Our friends have told us. We know what the score is. That's not the way it's going to be."

The teacher of the class indicated that he, too, thought the lesson did not make contact, because children's *feelings* about going to junior high school were ignored. The fears of the children should have been discussed. "Would they get beat up by older boys?" "Would their classes be noisy, out of order, and riotous?" "Would they get hurt?" "Would they be able to do the work?" The fears of these children, both real and irrational, could have been allayed if they had been expressed and if their validity had been examined through visits to the junior high school and through talks with junior high school personnel and students able to deal honestly with these concerns.

Class trips represent another situation which arouses the fears of some children. For example, one child, with total seriousness, remarked as his class discussed a forthcoming trip to Chinatown: "We've got to be careful of the food down there. They're liable to poison us." There are some children who always choose to remain behind when their classes go on trips. Others stay close to the teacher as they walk around in strange surroundings. Teachers can help to deal with these fears by acquainting themselves in as great detail as possible with what is going to happen and exactly where they are going, by presenting this information to the children, by arranging for other competent adult supervision, by informing the children of the ways in which their safety and care is to be assured, and by involving them in specific activity on the trip.

Many of the children reveal a deep interest in the subject of feelings. They are very much interested in knowing about such manifestations of feeling as fear, extreme worry, and anger. These are all phenomena they have either observed firsthand or experienced themselves with an intensity that is generally greater than that felt by children from middle-class areas. The children are amazed when they discover that there are actually words for feelings. "Hostility," "aggression," and "curiosity" all become meaningful terms when the teacher attaches these words to the emotions of children, when he displays pictures showing children in the throes of experiencing these emotions, and when the children themselves find pictures to illustrate these feelings.

When children have learned the words to identify particular emotions, they can better describe their reactions to stories. For example, after a reading of *Crow Boy* by Taro Yashima, children were able to react to a question, such as "How do you think Chibi felt being called stupid and slowpoke?" by relating the situation to their own comparable experiences. They were able to verbalize what the feelings of the main character in *Mary Jane* by Dorothy Sterling might have been when she was jostled by children in a newly integrated school.

With the atmosphere created by encouraging a free expression of feeling, children have written on such topics as "My First Day of School," "How I Felt on the Stage," and "Things that Make Me Angry." A child in a class where emotions had been identified and where they had been spoken of and written about, gave his feelings about his neighborhood:

What can I teach?

My block is the most terrible block I've ever seen. There are at least twenty-five or thirty narcotic people on my block. The cops come around there and tries to act bad but I bet inside of them they are as scared as can be. They even had in the papers that this block is the worst block, not in Manhattan but in New York City. In the summer they don't do nothing except shooting, stabing [sic], and fighting. They hang all over the stoops and when you say excuse me to them they hear you but they just don't feel like moving. Some times they make me so mad that I feel like slaping [sic] them and stuffing bag of garbage down their throats.

Successful teachers try to create situations that make for good feelings. With new children entering the class all during the year, they discuss such questions as: "How do you think someone new to our class feels?" "What can you do to make new children feel more comfortable?" "Why do fights start with new children?" As a result of these discussions, buddies are assigned to newcomers, after-school company for a walk to the library is provided, and the causes of fights are determined. Children feel good about their ability to "show someone around," and the newcomer feels less afraid of his new surroundings.

One teacher told of a child in her class who was going to the hospital for open-heart surgery. He seemed to want to tell about it, so the teacher suggested he talk to the class. John told about having a hole in his heart and the need for its repair. The children asked him many questions about his forthcoming operation. When he went to the hospital, the children wrote him letters which the teacher delivered personally. One letter contained a passage which reveals the straightforwardness of the children in expressing feeling. It read, in part, "You're such a nice boy, John. I hope you don't die." When John came home from the hospital, the children were eager to deliver homework assignments, books, and reports of classwork to him. Upon his return to class, he told the teacher his mother said he could

95

show her the operation. The teacher's calm, interested reaction to the view of a rather unsightly scar was communicated to the children when they, in turn, looked at the scar. The children realized why John couldn't participate in physical activity. They were aware of the need not to push or shove him. Thus a situation in which feelings of fear, strangeness, and difference were present was translated into an experience in which feelings of consideration, concern, and closeness were developed.

Other teachers have used the occasion of children's birthdays to develop good feelings by sending cards or by planning bulletin board displays which give recognition. Another method for helping children to have feelings of self-worth is to provide opportunities for every child to feel a sense of achievement. Even the child who may be weak academically can gain the spotlight if he is given the chance to display his bongo-playing ability, his knowledge of pigeon raising, his skill at sports, or his value as a member of the school audio-visual squad.

Many children in the ghetto have feelings of inferiority, low self-esteem, and ambivalent attitudes toward their own group. Almost every day provides examples to support the idea that many of the children are handicapped by deep feelings of lack of self-worth. For example, one day a Negro child, implying a mutual inferiority, said to a newly appointed Negro teacher, "They assigned you to our school because you're a Negro."

Another child, referring to the boycott of ghetto schools, remarked, "When the white children come to our school, everything will be better."

Negro teachers have expressed the idea that some of the children look up to white teachers and that some of the parents prefer white teachers for their children. Some children bristle with anger at the very mention of the word "Negro." As early as the third grade some children try to straighten their hair. The term "black" is frequently used as an epithet.

The inception of these feelings of self-deprecation is described in the following statement from the HARYOU Report, *Youth in the Ghetto:*

As minority group children learn the inferior status to which they are assigned and observe that they are usually segregated and isolated from the more privileged members of society, they react with deep feelings of inferiority and with a sense of personal humiliation. Many of them become confused about their personal worth. Like all other human beings, they require a sense of personal dignity and social support for positive self-esteem. Almost nowhere in the larger society, however, do they find their own dignity as human beings respected or protected. Under these conditions, minority-group children develop conflicts with regard to their feelings about themselves and about the value of the group with which they are identified. Understandably they begin to question whether they themselves and their group are worthy of no more respect from the larger society than they receive. These conflicts, confusions, and doubts give rise under certain circumstances to self-hatred and rejection of their own group.

The teacher in a ghetto elementary school must realize that the task of improving the self-image of the Negro child is a mammoth one, and that although it is the job of the total society to lift the crushing burden of prejudice and discrimination that contributes to self-deprecation, the teacher can do *something* to improve the image of the Negro child by helping to dissipate the notion that the Negro has made a negligible contribution to the cultural heritage of America.

A teacher described the situation as it existed in his class in this way:

There's so much the children don't know about their heritage and their culture. They haven't identified with their culture because they don't have any background information. Right now they look at the accomplishments of Negroes just as they would any success story, rather than as the achievements of someone

97

of their race whom they can emulate. They do identify more closely with sports heroes because they do know about Cassius Clay, Willie Mays, Floyd Patterson, and others.

Many teachers reported that the reading of poetry and stories written by Negroes didn't spark special interest. But when the teacher introduced such literature by relating it to the children's lives, he was able to stimulate curiosity about poems and stories derived from Negro culture. For example, a teacher told the children about the life of Langston Hughes. He indicated to them that the poet lived in a house very close to the school, that he got his ideas for his poems by walking down 125th Street or Lenox Avenue, and by looking to the life of the Negro in the South and in Africa. At other times the teacher read the children such poems as Langston Hughes's "Baby," and the children recalled the warnings of their own mothers to be careful of trucks in the street. The poem, "Ma Lord," also by Hughes, was reminiscent of the religious quality of many of the children's homes.

In another instance the teacher simply read "In the Morning" by Paul Laurence Dunbar, and the children responded with hilarity because the southern dialect used in the poem was so very real to them. It reminded them of their own experiences being rushed off to school in the morning.

Similarly, a reading of African myths and Negro folk tales can reveal to children the wit, wisdom, and philosophy of people who traditionally have used storytelling as a way of relaxing after a day's toil and as a means of explaining life's mysteries. The imaginative teacher can simulate the setting of a group of people around a fire eagerly listening to a gifted storyteller spinning his tale.

(The Appendix includes a list of books about the American Negro which the teacher may use to provide many moments of enjoyment and to help children develop greater pride in the contributions of their culture.)

98

Children in the ghetto have little understanding of Negro history. For example, in one class the teacher told the story of Crispus Attucks, a Negro who was the first American to die in the Revolutionary War. The children were surprised by this information, because they thought all Negroes were slaves working on southern plantations.

Since greater emphasis needs to be given to the role of the Negro in American cultural development, it is incumbent upon the teacher to become knowledgeable in this area. The teacher who recognizes the impact of the Negro upon American culture can help his pupils gain a more complete picture of American historical development. For example, a study of the Civil War can include investigation into the lives of such people as Frederick Douglass, Robert Smalls, and Harriet Tubman. When children study an ant colony at work, they can, as part of their inquiry, find out about Charles Turner and his study of ants. Poetry programs can be made up, in part, of the works of such poets as James Weldon Johnson, Phillis Wheatley, and Countee Cullen. As part of a program of rhythmic activities, children can imitate John Henry swinging his mighty hammer. In music they can sing such songs as "Blue-Tail Fly," "Skip to My Lou," and "Shoo-Fly," and such spirituals as "Let Us Break Bread Together" and "Go Down Moses." Studies of occupations can be made more vital by visits from Negroes holding different kinds of jobs. Bulletin board displays can include pictures of Negroes as well as those of whites. Current events discussions cannot realistically omit reports of the many outstanding Negroes in public life. The teacher can aim to introduce the contributions of the Negro culture in a manner that presents a balanced, accurate picture of the Negro in American life.

Some admonitions are in order. The achievements of minority-group members must be kept in perspective; if the achievements are exaggerated, they create the impression that the individuals are anomalies. For example, after an isolated study of Negro history, one child asked, "Are there only famous Negro people?"

To emphasize achievements solely because of blood strain is to make the error of attributing accomplishment to inherent racial qualities. For example, it would be fallacious to cite the works of Alexander Dumas, who was of Negro ancestry, as an instance of Negro achievement, because his contributions were an outgrowth of his contact with French culture rather than with Negro culture.

Negro History Week celebrations which focus primarily on the accomplishments of Negroes in the fields of sports and entertainment tend to stress an extremely limited contribution to the American heritage. The very limitation of a single week to a study of Negro history is patronizing in nature. As Langston Hughes put it, "If there is to be a Negro History Week, why not also have a White History Week?"

When children learn that members of the Negro race have made and are making important contributions to the development of American culture, they can begin to attach a sense of value to their group. Similarly, if Negro children are given an accurate picture of their earliest ancestry in Africa, they can begin to feel a sense of pride in their past and to see themselves as part of a group that is worthy of respect.

Africa has a rich background in history, poetry, folklore, games, and song, all of which can easily interest children. In addition, Africa today is the scene of change, and the story of changing conditions is a story with which the children, with their own hopes for an improved life, can easily identify. Africa, with its burgeoning nations, is achieving an importance that demands the attention of a school that seeks to present an accurate picture of the world today.

The history of Africa's early civilizations has been virtually omitted from the textbooks and curricula of schools of every level, from elementary to college. Booker T. Washington wrote of his own reaction as a child to the neglect and distortion of African life:

> As I recall my first definite impressions of my race in Africa, the books I read as a boy always put the pictures of Africa and African life in an unnecessarily cruel contrast with the pictures of the civilized and highly cultured Europeans and Americans. One picture I recall vividly was in the first geography I studied. It was the picture of George Washington placed side by side with a naked African having a ring in his nose and a dagger in his hand.

The teacher who informs himself can help to clear away distortion and break the long spell of silence that has existed. Children can learn about such advanced civilizations as those of Ghana, Nigeria, and Mali. They can be exposed to samples of African folklore which attempt to explain natural phenomena, pose dilemmas, and use animals as the main characters. They can hear the wisdom of such African proverbs as "A roaring lion kills no game," "He who goes with a wolf will learn to howl," and "When the rat laughs at the cat, there is a hole." They can find out about the games African children play. They can see which of these games they are familiar with and learn to play some that are strange to them. They can learn African songs and see samples of African art. They can follow news developments that concern Africa.

The teacher who leads his class into a study of Africa, past and present, brings the children closer to a part of the globe that is an integral part of today's world, and helps them to find in their past reasons for pride in their race.

EXPLORING THE CHILDREN'S WORLD

The world of many depressed-area elementary school children is a world of confusion, a world of ignorance of abstract institutions, a world of physical limitation, a world of stereotypes.

101

A handbook for teaching in the ghetto school

It is a world where civil rights groups have been active, where school boycotts have been effective, where word of black nationalist activity has been heard, and where the result of all this has been confusion for many elementary schoolchildren.

It is a world where many families live on Department of Welfare checks—yet where the children hardly know who pays for their welfare, what checks are, and why welfare is necessary.

It is a world whose boundaries are restricted by fear of physical harm and of strange surroundings. A few square blocks may comprise the entire life space of a child. Information from the outside seeps in from television, movies, and adult conversation.

It is a world where limited experience often causes children to see stereotypes rather than individuals.

The question of civil rights. The ghetto is a world in turmoil. Children and parents in the slum community are bombarded by reports of inferior education, plans for boycotts and other forms of protest, and stories of southern violence against Negroes. In many ways the Negro ghetto is the direct center of society's attempt to deal with its most pressing problem.

A teacher needs to use good judgment in placing the ponderous, mammoth problems of society on the shoulders of children, but at the same time he needs to help children learn about what is going on around them. Since civil rights activities, in general, and the school integration issue, in particular, directly involve the children in ghetto-area schools, the teacher should examine these issues in the classroom so that, as far as possible, distortion may be replaced with fact and superficial thinking may give way to insight.

A prerequisite to dealing effectively with the school integration issue is an understanding of all aspects of the question. The teacher should be fully aware of proposed methods for dealing with the problem of racial imbalance. He must understand the meaning and implication of such methods as Open Enrollment, the Free-Choice Transfer Policy, the Princeton Plan, Site Selection, redistricting, transfer of children from over-crowded to underutilized schools, and reverse busing. He must stay in touch with attempts to raise the educational level of all children. Such attempts include the Higher Horizons Program, the After-School Tutorial Program, the More Effective Schools program, and the pre-kindergarten program. He should be aware of the fears of the white community—that the neighborhood school concept will be destroyed, that the movement of Negro children into white schools will lower educational standards and achievement, and that contact with slum children will be bad for white middle-class children. He must try to identify with the frustrations of a people who see their children not achieving, whose children often have the most inexperienced teachers, and who sense that a segregated education is an inferior education.

Children will react to contemporary issues in a confused manner when they have had little preparation in learning how to deal with current events. That this was so in relation to the New York City school boycott is indicated by the following teacher observations:

"The children didn't know why they stayed out of school on the day of the boycott. It was just a day off for most of them."

"The children are confused by the civil rights movement. They feel the turmoil. They don't know how to let it out."

"The school boycott had an adverse effect. It gave the children the idea that everybody's fighting for them. They feel that they don't have to do anything themselves. The children also saw adults breaking the law."

"The boycott increased the animosity toward the school."

The children need guidance in learning to read newspapers, in listening to radio programs, in conducting panel discussions, in seeing the many sides of an issue, and in differentiating between fact and opinion. Listing "facts" and "opinions" surrounding an issue on the blackboard can be useful. Role-playing can be valuable in that it can help children see and feel opposing viewpoints. It is advisable in discussions that ground rules be formulated to include the citing of sources for facts and to rule out name-calling.

Astute handling of "hot" issues demands a teacher who has succeeded in developing a classroom where honest expression is encouraged, a teacher who is skilled in conducting group discussions. One teacher discussed her manner of dealing with such issues as integration, civil rights, and school boycotts:

> The day after the school boycott I sensed that the children were shy, kind of afraid. After all, they had stayed out of school, and all their school careers they've been told that they had to be in school unless they were sick. The children were concerned about my reaction to their absence. But when I asked questions about what they had done at the Freedom Schools, they felt more at ease. I did not condemn them for not being in school.
>
> We discussed why the boycott was being held. We learned about the leaders of the various groups. Letters were written to some of these leaders seeking responses to questions that came up. We listed the arguments in favor of and opposed to the school boycott. The reasons why children did not attend school were indicated. We talked about the values to be gained from integrated schools. We considered how they might feel going to a school where white children were in the majority or in having white children come to their school.
>
> In discussions of this sort I try very hard not to moralize. I try to deal with the confusion in the minds of the children. I know that they're mixed up between what they hear at home and in the community about inferior teachers and their allegiance to me. I know they're mixed up by the anger they hear expressed towards whites and the fact that I'm white. I know it's hard for them to talk about these things at all. I remember how when I first brought up the situation in Mississippi, no one wanted to

talk. Finally, one child very hesitantly mentioned that a Negro had been attacked by whites. When they truly felt that I not only listened but actually encouraged them to talk, then the questions flew thick and fast.

"Why do white people hit Negro people?"

"My mother says when somebody hits you, you should hit back. How come the Negro people that I see on television just let white people hit them and don't hit back?"

"Why do Negroes always have trouble?"

"Why do white people hate Negroes?"

"Why were Negro people slaves?"

Questions came up that I couldn't answer, but at least they came up.

The teacher will probably find that the children are reluctant to talk about the civil rights movement and their relation to it as Negro children, because they sense it is a forbidden subject: anger toward white institutions and toward the school. The anger has been communicated to them by their parents and by the community. But if the teacher encourages them to talk and doesn't moralize, the children will feel freer to express their concern and confusion, and the way to clearer understanding may be opened.

City agencies that affect children's lives. The Department of Welfare affects the lives of many of the children. But how this agency works and how to deal with it are problems beyond the scope not only of the children but of most of the people of the community.

Many of the children live in houses that abound in violations of the city's housing and health codes. Inadequate heating, unsanitary plumbing, fire hazards, and inept maintenance are a part of their daily existence. Most of the families who live with the cold drafts, the scurrying of rats, the threat of fire, and the darkness of burned-out hallway bulbs feel incapable of finding help to make changes.

A handbook for teaching in the ghetto school

Each school day children in ghetto areas walk by houses whose shattered frameworks and jagged windows speak loudly of the past terror and dislocation of families who have been burned out. Injury or illness will likely bring a child to the emergency clinic of the nearest hospital. Policemen direct traffic, pursue law violators, and apprehend suspicious characters all within full view of the children. Such city agencies as the Fire Department, the Department of Hospitals, the Police Department, the Department of Welfare, and the Building Department concentrate much of their activity in the ghetto, and yet the people who come to carry out their functions as members of these agencies appear to the community as men from another planet. The children see city departments as giant, bloodless beings.

If the elementary schools in the ghetto are to help children develop any kind of mastery over their environment, the children must be helped to understand the functions of city agencies, their manner of operation, and the ways in which individuals can establish contact with them.

One teacher sought to dissipate the children's vagueness about the operations of the Department of Welfare. He had checks copied, and the children learned to fill them out. They learned what a check represents, what proper care of a check involves, and why they are used. They discussed how checks are endorsed and how they can be cashed. They talked about various kinds of checks, such as teacher salary checks, tax refund checks, and welfare checks. They gained some idea of where the money comes from to back up these checks. As incidents occurred in the community, as they do inevitably, other services of the Department of Welfare became apparent. The children became aware that families whose homes were burned out were provided temporary shelter by the Department of Welfare, and that families who were without suitable home guidance due

106

to parent illness or other disposition were given the services of a homemaker. The concept of surplus food was clarified as children discussed the kinds of food that comprise surplus and the origin of such foods. Samples of the foods were examined. The variety of ways in which these foods could be used was investigated. The class saw how a lack of employment made welfare a necessary city service.

The children began to recognize that a city is made up of people. It is farmers selling surplus food to the government, men distributing it at central locations, women helping sick or working mothers to care for small children, people paying taxes to assist others as they seek employment, doctors helping children to get well. All this has to be communicated without any sign of deprecation or sympathy if the teaching is to be effective.

Other recurring events make possible a study of the Housing Authority. Children leave the school and the neighborhood because their families have been admitted to housing projects. It can then become feasible to discuss with the children how people get into housing projects, what housing projects are like, who builds and manages them, and how people feel about going to live in a project.

Poor housing conditions have resulted in rent strikes. As part of current events discussions, children can describe the conditions that have led to this type of protest. They can find out what the standards of healthful housing should be. They can investigate what responsibilities city agencies have in seeing that these standards are maintained. They can find out who the appropriate authorities are and how to inform them of violations. (Correct letter writing form and courteous telephone manners can be introduced at the same time.) Children can role-play telephone conversations and interviews whose focus is to report housing defects.

Children can thus learn that there are agencies responsible for seeing to it that healthful housing conditions are maintained. They can learn to use these agencies and other channels of protest without hesitation.

Other real situations can suggest discussions of different city agencies. For example, directly opposite an elementary school in East Harlem two burned-out houses stand as vivid testimony to the destruction wrought by fire. With this kind of striking example before them, a class's attention can be directed to a study of the work of the Fire Department. A trip to the fire house can illustrate how the Fire Department operates. A fireman who visits the school can indicate the common causes of fires in the neighborhood, the danger and expense involved in false alarms, and the appropriate steps in reporting a fire. He can tell the children about the qualifications needed for the job of fireman. The different types of fire-fighting equipment can be described. Children can learn about the various jobs in the department and the functions they serve.

The community hospital is a place children can visit to learn more about the services provided by city hospitals. They can see where the ambulances leave from; they can talk to the ambulance drivers; they can visit the laboratories; they can observe doctors and nurses at work. They can take a trip to the nurses' training center and talk to the girls about the preparation they are receiving. The children can learn about the operation of mobile X-ray units that are seen in the community. They can find out what X-ray technicians do and what X-rays reveal. As they talk to the people involved, visit health centers, and read about hospitals, the children can develop a closer familiarity with the system of city health and hospital care.

More informal contacts with members of the Police Department are needed if hostile attitudes are to be modified and if the children are to become better acquainted with the Police

Department's role as a service to the community. Policemen can visit the school to talk about the importance of obeying safety regulations, the need for cooperating with the corner policeman, and the kind of training needed for the job of policeman. Through trips to the police station, children can learn about other aspects of police work, such as crime detection, emergency rescues, and naval operations.

The problem of developing a broader understanding of the Police Department is usually complicated by the poor relationship that exists between the community and the department. Candid questions involved in this problem can help children gain a clearer, more balanced view of the situation. The children can consider such questions as: "Why don't all people report crimes to the police?" "How do you think policemen feel about charges of brutality?" "Why do some people dislike the police?" "How do you think the police feel when they think the people don't like them?" "How can the people in the neighborhood and the police grow to understand each other better?" Despite the problems that exist, it is possible to begin to develop a more accurate picture of the services provided by the Police Department.

Children are in daily contact with other city agencies. They include the Park Department, the Department of Sanitation, the Rapid Transit System, the Department of Gas and Electricity, and the Department of Water Supply. By focusing on the work of city agencies, by arranging for more personal contact with these agencies, and by exploring in depth the effect of agency work, the school can help the children develop a clearer understanding of this aspect of the world around them.

Other people, other communities. The physical world of many children in depressed areas is a matter of blocks, for they are afraid to venture into strange surroundings. In addition, most of them have not had the experience of being taken to other

109

parts of the city except to visit relatives or friends in other ghetto areas. They have had almost no contact with children and adults from other communities.

As a result of this limited exposure the children's picture of other people and other communities is very often either distorted or totally nonexistent. For example, one result of publicity regarding the so-called better white schools was to reinforce a view held by Negro children of white children and their families. The idea expressed by many of the Negro children was that all white children come from wealthy families. The remark of another child also reveals a misconception resulting from insular contacts. He asked: "Is President Johnson a Negro? He speaks with a southern accent."

Other distortions prevail because children have, like the blind men touching the elephant, seen only a portion of reality. Many children think that all-white neighborhoods are made up of clean, comfortable-looking one-family houses with neatly kept lawns. The children see storekeepers as angry, suspicious men who are always wary of children taking things. This last distortion was illustrated when two young men whom the children knew and spoke to daily on the street corner opened a store. The children's relationships with them in the confines of the store suddenly became reticent and defensive.

The children are living in a world where cracks are beginning to show in the walls of the ghetto. Hopefully, these cracks will widen and the walls will eventually crumble. If conflict is to give way to amity, if cooperation is to replace debilitating competition, and if respect rather than deprecation or envy is to be the tone of the times, then the children must be helped to see other people and other places as they really are and not as stereotypes. The most logical place to start is with the immediacy of the child's own city.

Negro children can learn about white children when they have contact with them. A white Jewish girl joined a third-grade class in Harlem. During the course of the year she told about going to a Hebrew school and found out about the religious schools her classmates attended. She described her neighborhood, learned about the neighborhood surrounding the school community, invited children to her house, and visited children in their homes.

Another instance of intermingling of cultures has occurred when the children of white teachers have visited the school. A barrage of curious questions inevitably resulted.

A teacher in a school of Negro children can establish a relationship between his class and one in a white neighborhood school. Children can exchange letters telling of such things as allowance money, clothes, movies, houses, favorite foods, and problems with brothers and sisters. If contact is initiated with a class in a school in a poor neighborhood, the children can learn that not all white children are rich, that they have many of the same problems, and that they have many of the same likes and dislikes. Exchanges of photographs, schoolwork, tape recordings, and actual visits can bring children a closer knowledge of each other.

The film *Let Us Break Bread Together* (available from the Bureau of Audiovisual Instruction of the New York City Board of Education) tells the story of how the children and parents in two outwardly different schools planned and participated in such activities as assemblies and field days. In this way both children and parents began to see each other more as human beings than as members of different races.

Another way to help dispel the notion that all white children come from well-to-do families is for the children to participate in a drive to help white poverty-stricken Appalachian families. Pennies can be saved and collected, and the children can feel the pleasure of giving as opposed to the uneasiness that comes of always being on the receiving end.

Meetings with other people can help to broaden the children's view of their city and the people in it. A teacher's friend, an emigrant from Jamaica, came to play the piano for the children. They were fascinated not only by his playing but by the clipped accent of his Jamaican speech. Another teacher had a Negro sculptor friend come to school to display and demonstrate her work to the children. The cultivated quality of her speech, shaped as it was in part by her eastern college education, was in sharp contrast to the Jamaican English.

Both visitors described why they spoke the way they did. The Jamaican told some of the history of his island and of the many British influences that exist there. The sculptor indicated her southern origin and how, as a young child, she had traces of a southern accent which she lost through education and contact with people who spoke in a different way.

Both tried to show how they reached to their roots to express themselves, how they saw beauty in such things as calypso rhythms and the face of an old Negro slave woman. Both exemplified Negroes who differed sharply in speech, profession, and education from most of the Negroes whom the children knew.

Audio-visual materials can be put to effective use. Teachers can plan to have the children listen to tape-recorded samples of English as it is spoken by Negroes and whites from various parts of the globe. A Negro from the British West Indies and a white man from London might sound very much alike. The speech of Diana Sands and Shelley Winters might both be tinged with a New York accent, but the difference in race would not be visible. A comparison of the voices of President Johnson and Paul Robeson would show the difference between northern and southern speech, not the difference between a white and black man's speech. The notion that equates a southern accent with being a Negro can be dissipated as children are made aware of the variety of speech patterns that exist among all races.

Television can help to avert the tendency to overgeneralize. Children who see a United Nations session on television are likely to become aware of Negroes who speak French, Spanish, and Portuguese, as well as English. Seeing and hearing such Negroes as James Baldwin, Ossie Davis, Bayard Rustin, Roy Wilkins, and James Farmer can do much to present the children with models of speech and humanity which they have not previously known.

Bulletin board displays of pictures of the children of different races who live in the city can give Negro children an identification with their own race and a recognition that America is made up of many races. Today's newspaper advertisements can be used as a source of pictures since they have changed to include models of different racial backgrounds. Pictures of life in other communities within the city can be collected for inclusion in a scrapbook. A systematic survey of the daily newspaper and national magazines can yield a harvest of pictures of city life.

Trips can be invaluable for children whose movements out of their own neighborhood have been minimal. A trip to Chinatown for one class acquainted them with a pagoda telephone booth, a Chinese temple, and Chinese people. Another class went to Radio City, visited an automat, and exchanged words with friendly adults. Trips such as these introduce children to the various forms of transportation that are available to people in the city. An excursion to Staten Island gave the joy of a brief "ocean" voyage and a look at a community totally different from Harlem.

For one group of segregated Negro children, walks just beyond the borders of the immediate school community brought them into contact with a community center that is as well equipped as any. Within ten minutes of their school the children saw Italian people and stores advertising Italian foods, and heard Italian spoken. This walk permitted the children a view of

113

the majestic splendor of the Triboro Bridge. They walked into stores that have no bars covering the windows and no wire screens shielding their owners.

The children's knowledge of the city can develop as they make maps that depict such occupational centers as the Fulton Fish Market, the flower market, and the garment center. They can construct different maps showing museums, places of interest, recreation centers, bridges, and tunnels. They can plan bus and subway trips to various parts of the city. They can gather factual materials to help them plan trips for imaginary visitors to the city.

Children can be helped to develop an empathy for other segments of the city's population as they make plans for class celebrations to coincide with the Chinese New Year, the Jewish New Year, and the Greek Epiphany. Samples of foods of different national origin can be introduced into the classroom. Displays of foreign-language newspapers and of menus from foreign restaurants can give an idea of the polyglot composition of a large city's population. The songs and dances of other nations can easily be made part of the school's assembly and physical education programs.

The teacher has a wealth of material at hand to help children dissipate stereotypes and see the vast possibilities for enjoyment that lie in the rich complexity of the city and its people.

6 What materials can help?

Elementary schoolteachers in the ghetto have expressed the idea that children in their classes learn best through visual and tactile approaches which involve them totally. Their findings support research that has demonstrated that passive spectatorship does not make for optimum learning. They lend credence to the idea that the use of visual and manipulative materials, at least in the initial stages, is more likely to involve children from low socioeconomic areas. But teachers also emphasize the continuing need for instruction to develop the children's listening abilities so that auditory teaching approaches may be more effective.

The education of depressed-area children *outside* of school is real and firsthand. The relationship to abstract exchange is miniscule. If the teacher relies mainly on abstract presentations through verbalization, it is unlikely that the children will ever absorb organized knowledge or realize its value in meeting their own life problems.

The teacher who wants to make contact with the children in his classes should be acquainted with the types of materials that have proved effective. It is essential, however, to remember that the materials used in a classroom represent only one aspect of the teaching-learning situation. By themselves they do little. To be useful they must be part of a class learning situation where a positive feeling tone exists. To be of value the materials must be used not in isolation but in connection with a continuous flow of learning experiences. For example, one teacher, in describing how she planned to use a filmstrip, said: "I'll read a story to the children that I know will catch their interest. Then I'll show a filmstrip which relates to the story, and then I'll have sections of the story copied for children to use as reading material."

Another point for teachers to keep in mind is that useful materials must not be those with which the children have formerly experienced continual failure.

REXOGRAPH MATERIALS

Successful teachers rely greatly on rexographed material and have indicated its many values. Among these are the facts that it can be geared to diagnosed needs, that it is concrete, that it represents a personal type of instruction in that the children interpret it as something the teacher has done especially for them, and that it can act as a bond with the home.

Teachers have used rexographed material for many purposes. Some teachers have initiated the year's activities by rexographing a letter of welcome to parents which also indicates the class's homework policy, the suggested role of the parent in preparing the child for school, the need for notes to explain lateness or absence, and when the teacher will be available for meetings with parents. Contacts with parents are maintained throughout the year as letters regarding trip plans are composed, rexographed, and sent home. Children's stories can be rexographed, stapled together, and made available to parents as representative samples of work done in school.

Rexographed material has been used for homework purposes, too. For example, children in a sixth-grade class were given a blank rexograph time budget on which to indicate how they spent their time after school hours. This helped them to select hours for study. One teacher used rexographed material to guide children's viewing of a television program. She gave them the assignment of watching the film, *Huckleberry Finn,* on television and of answering such questions as: "How do you think Huck felt about living in the Widow Douglas' home?" "Why do you think he felt that way?" Practice material in mathematics and language has often been rexographed.

Teachers have rexographed material for direct classroom instruction in many areas. Stories that will interest children are duplicated and used to improve children's comprehension ability. Guides for proofreading are discussed, taught, duplicated, and distributed to children for reference. Maps of the community and of the school are composed and rexographed to help orient children to their surroundings. Original material made up by the teacher or material chosen from workbooks is rexographed for children to use as a means of caring for diagnosed needs. Short class quizzes are presented in rexographed form. Pictorial representation of mathematics materials gives children another form of concrete learning. Colorfully organized crossword puzzles have been used to help develop concepts. The completion of these puzzles brings satisfaction to the children, and the puzzle itself makes for a specific structure in which the child can operate. One teacher used the children's interest in jobs to make up an illustrated puzzle that included such clues as:

117

A handbook for teaching in the ghetto school

"If you like horses, you would enjoy working in a
      store   rodeo."

Many teachers reported using the words to songs to help children develop their reading abilities and gain an understanding of the rich heritage of music that is part of Negro culture. Such songs as "The Blue-Tail Fly," "Polly-Wolly-Doodle," "O, Desayo!," "Lift Every Voice and Sing," and "Chain Gang" were duplicated and used for singing, reading, and understanding the culture and time from which they came. Children's personal collections of those songs became an important source of enjoyment and reading material. Likewise, in the fifth and sixth grades, such poems as Paul Laurence Dunbar's "In the Morning," James Weldon Johnson's "The Creation," and Langston Hughes's "Ennui" and "I Have Known Rivers" were duplicated, read, discussed, and enjoyed.

Teachers have helped children learn the importance of following directions carefully by having them pay close attention to rexographed directions. For example, one teacher worked with his group of children to make their own books. These directions were then listed, rexographed, and made available to all children for future use.

Children can also be given the experience of working with rexograph stencils. One teacher encouraged her children to make up their own reading progress charts. Each child prepared his own rexographed sheet and was allowed to run it off by himself. Many opportunities can be found for children to rexograph materials for themselves and for other children as well.

Rexographed material has particular value for children in ghetto elementary schools in that it is concrete, it can be geared to individual needs, it is personal in that it becomes the property of each child, it is lasting because the child has continual recourse to it, and it enables the child to inform his parent of what he is doing in school.

118

WORKBOOKS

Intelligent use of workbooks has enabled teachers to present clearly defined tasks which are geared to the ability levels of the children. For example, teachers have used single copies of workbooks to care for individual needs and to encourage children to work independently at helping themselves. These teachers have gleaned from various workbooks material designed to help children with specific reading skills. Pages have been organized in separate boxes, and on each box a specific skill is indicated. The correct answers to questions are placed on the back of the pages, which are arranged in order of difficulty. The teacher helps the child become aware of the skill in which he needs more practice. In this way children can select appropriate material for individual self-help.

Workbooks also have the value of being personal, in that each child has his own particular property. Since possessions are so important to depressed-area children, it is helpful when workbooks are considered expendable and are given to children for use during the year. Teachers have indicated that when a child has his own workbook, when he can work in it, take it home, and see it checked by the teacher, much learning and satisfaction results. Despite the fact that there is a need for better workbooks, those available can provide structure, the satisfaction of success, and the material to help with instruction in areas of need.

FILMSTRIPS

Teachers report that the appeal to the visual sense makes for an immediate stimulus to discussion. The darkened classroom and the screen picture stimulus sometimes combine to encourage otherwise reticent students to express themselves orally. The filmstrip provides unusual opportunities to help students to learn to verbalize about what they see—an essential activity for children who have had so little practice in doing this. It helps children gain a visual understanding of abstract concepts. It permits the teacher an added opportunity to diagnose reading skills and gives children a chance to develop greater understanding of word symbols and vocabulary concepts. It makes for a situation in which the entire group focuses on a lighted screen and learns together as explanations of the filmstrip material are presented.

TELEVISION

Teachers have reported some use of television as a material of instruction. They have used home viewing as a source of homework assignments. Children have been asked to watch programs on pioneer life as an aid to a class study of westward expansion. They have been asked to look at news broadcasts to learn about current happenings. Teachers have directed children's attention to good films and special programs.

An evaluation by teachers of the educational television programs viewed in one ghetto elementary school indicated that the novelty of television in school made for initial interest on the part of the children. But very often the programs had no direct connection to the lives of the children or to what they were learning in school at the time. Moreover, the verbal level used was too difficult for the children to understand. This evaluation indicates the need for teachers to investigate the content and quality of a television program before including it as part of their class work, and to consider what questions and activities can result from the program.

FLAT PICTURES

Teachers have used flat picture materials to create an attractive

120

room. Colorful pictures tastefully mounted have helped children develop a pride in *their* room. The need to use pictures of Negro children and adults cannot be overemphasized. *Ebony* has become a "must" subscription for schools in ghetto areas, for it provides a great fund of pictures which use Negroes as subjects.

Pictures have proved especially valuable in working with poor readers. As one teacher said in describing her approach with slow children, "I don't tell them. I show them." For example, to attempt to clarify verbally the term "prairie schooner" for a fifth-grade class of slow children is an almost impossible task. However, when children who have been taught picture analysis skills have had a chance to see pictures of ocean schooners, they can then study pictures of prairie schooners and see the suitability of the term "schooner" in the context of land travel.

Children have been asked to compose captions for pictures, to indicate what they see in pictures, and to choose pictures for bulletin boards or scrapbooks. They have been asked to find pictures that illustrate concepts, phonic blends, and chronology. For example, children can learn about sequence by arranging pictures of tadpoles and frogs in their order of development.

Pictures have been used to help children express feeling, too. Pictures of other children in unique poses of expression help children recall their own feelings and experiences. Questions such as "How do you think the boy in the picture feels?" "Why do you think he feels that way?" and "When have you ever felt that way?" can make for expression of feeling and lead to worthwhile creative writing.

Teachers think children learn best from and prefer pictures that are meaningful to them. Pictures of television and cartoon characters are part of the real experience of children and as such stimulate their interest.

The teacher who has a classroom picture file with such headings as Negro History, Negroes in the News, Pictures of Negroes, Pictures to Evoke Feeling, Famous Americans, Pictures of

A handbook for teaching in the ghetto school

Foods, Pictures for Phonics, Pictures of Space Exploration, etc., has an important teaching tool.

OPAQUE PROJECTOR

The opaque projector also has been used effectively by teachers. It has been used to help children learn the words to songs, or for close study of flat pictures. One teacher used it as part of an assembly program in which children's illustrations were flashed on a screen to coincide with the telling of a story. On other occasions samples of children's art work were shared through the use of the opaque projector.

OVERHEAD PROJECTOR

The use of the overhead projector has several important advantages. The projector is sufficiently powerful to permit successful operation in a lighted room, and the teacher can maintain closer contact with the class because he can face his audience as he operates the machine. Another advantage is that the teacher can point out features appearing on the screen by pointing to the materials on the projector itself.

REALIA

It is the consensus of successful teachers in ghetto elementary schools that the children learn better through working with concrete objects than with abstract symbols. Therefore they use real things to give substance to learning experience. For example, the teletrainer provided by the New York Telephone Company has helped children to work on good speech and courteous, effective use of the telephone. The telephones in the teletrainer unit actually work, giving off dial tones, busy signals, and amplifying the conversation for the whole class to hear.

122

Living things in the classroom can also be a source of much fascination and learning. Fish, hamsters, pet alligators, and plants all invariably involve the children, providing the impetus for further study and investigation. Collections of rocks, insects, leaves, and pressed flowers are likewise a source of great interest because they, too, permit handling and close viewing.

MATHEMATICS MATERIALS

When dealing with mathematics, teachers have made use of manipulative materials to help children develop a better understanding of abstract mathematical symbols. Pegs, discs, tens frames, place-value cards, abacuses, squared material, fractional parts, and flannel boards are examples of representative materials used. Rulers, clocks, coins, stamps, tickets, scales, bottles, and thermometers are examples of real materials which have been used to relate to the mathematical experiences of children.

GAMES AND PUZZLES

Games and puzzles afford the satisfaction of solutions that are immediately visible. Matching word cards, finding the correct sequence of sentences printed on separate pieces of oaktag, doing anagrams, and playing word bingo are examples of activities used in many classrooms. One teacher found that such games as checkers, dominoes, and chess had great value. They helped children learn things besides the technical aspects of the games—that it is necessary to wait your turn, that there are strengths other than physical (exemplified by a tiny, frail-looking boy who was the master checker player of the class), and that one must think ahead in order to be a successful player. The teacher was able to apply this last idea to problem-solving in mathematics. He reminded the children of how they analyzed moves in checkers and pointed out the necessity for doing the same in solving mathematical problems.

A handbook for teaching in the ghetto school

CRAFT MATERIALS

Craft materials allow the children to experience the satisfaction of personal workmanship. They give children the chance to explore and learn about the properties of various materials. They help to develop patterns of creative expression which make constructive use of the children's emotional and mental energy. They provide the relaxation of a highly structured, simple activity. Some teachers described their use of lanyard material and looms primarily as a means of giving the children the satisfaction of the completed product and the comfort of a well-defined, easy operation. Another teacher achieved similar results by having the children make clay dishes and ash trays which were then hardened in the school kiln.

RECORDS

Records have been put to varied uses by teachers. One teacher always had quiet music playing when the children entered the room as a way of creating a soothing atmosphere. Other teachers have used records to help develop more acute listening habits for the children. They asked the children to listen for particular instruments or special effects in a musical selection. Another teacher indicated that certain folk music elicited the most interest. For example, chain gang music, which is part of the mythology of the ghetto, evoked much discussion from a group of sixth-graders.

EXPERIENCE CHARTS

Almost every teacher interviewed spoke of experience charts. Through their use, children connected their verbal comments with the written word. Slow readers were able to develop their own personal reading material by dictating stories which were recorded by the teacher. In this manner they were led to see that words could be found to describe their personal experiences. Word lists, unique because they were personal to each child, were made up. Teachers have also used experience charts to review observations made on trips, to stress directions for class routines, and to list questions in curriculum areas.

DRAMATIZATION MATERIALS

Because children in the ghetto attend closely to the performances of their peers, there is much potential value in dramatization materials. One vivid illustration occurred when a group of children acted out "In the Morning" by Paul Laurence Dunbar. They were taken by the reality of the situation in which a child was getting ready for school. Hilarity swept the audience as the child who was playing the father said to the slow-moving schoolboy, "I'm going to whup you if you don't get a move on." It was a familiar phrase in a familiar setting.

LISTENING MATERIALS

Those materials that appeal primarily to the visual and tactile senses have met with the greatest initial success. But this is not to negate the use of materials which attempt to develop auditory sensitivity. For example, teachers have reported using to good advantage such materials as the Listening Skill Builders of the SRA Reading Laboratory, which consist of a story or article to be presented to the class and follow-up exercises which check pupils' ability to recall main ideas, to note important details, and to pay attention to the sequence of events in the story.

Music can be helpful in teaching auditory discrimination, too. The familiar "Old MacDonald Had a Farm" can help children in the primary grades to notice the differences among the vowel sounds "e," "i," and "o."

Some primary-grade teachers have pre-recorded tapes to help develop auditory discrimination. The tapes are used with illustrated material. The teacher's voice asks the children questions about the prepared material; the children, all of whom have earphones, respond out loud to the questions, and the taped voice indicates if the answers are correct. Usually three children at a time move to a listening area for this independent practice.

Teachers have frequently used story-reading or storytelling to improve children's listening. Children can be asked to retell the story in their own words, to react to incidents in the story, and to participate in chanting story refrains. Choral speaking materials, too, can help to develop listening ability; as the group strives for a common effect, the children become sensitive to stress or pronunciations which mar the reading.

Although materials which emphasize a pictorial or tactile approach generally make a greater first impression, the teacher should not neglect materials which will help to develop auditory sensitivity.

7 What is the community like?

Ghetto communities differ in various ways, but it is striking to note their many similarities. Deteriorating housing, lack of play space, one-parent homes, an unskilled working population, and an apparently apathetic adult group are generally characteristic of all slum communities. What follows is a picture of a community surrounding an elementary school in East Harlem. An examination of this community may be helpful for the teacher in any depressed-area elementary school, because many of the characteristics portrayed are likely to be found in all ghetto communities and to have a significant effect on the school.

Public School 79 is located on Madison Avenue between 120th and 121st Streets. With its play area it covers a complete city block. It was opened for use in February 1963. The newness of the structure stands in sharp contrast to the weather-beaten, dirty-clay look of the dwellings on the blocks around it. There seem to be no efforts to improve housing, and the ravages of time and accident continue to gnaw away at the structures. Two buildings opposite the school, which were beset by fire, have now stood for over a year with jagged windows, gaping holes in the brick sides, and open-door entrances. They have become play areas for the more adventurous children and convenient hideaways for narcotics addicts.

Because the new school building is not large enough to care for all the children who attended the old school, the former P.S. 103 has remained in existence on 119th Street and Madison Avenue. This five-story structure was built in 1894 and now is used for the school's third-grade classes. Cooper Junior High School, on the west side of Madison Avenue, uses the top floor of the building for its seventh-grade girls.

The eastern boundary of P.S. 79's district is the New York Central elevated track which runs on Park Avenue to 96th Street. This fact, on occasion, demands that teachers whose classrooms face Park Avenue pause as the sound of passing trains interferes with teaching.

The northern boundary line is 122nd Street and runs only one block from Madison Avenue to Park Avenue. This square block area includes housing which is a cut above the rest of the housing in the school district. For one thing, it is an area without any small business establishments, a factor that contributes to its residential quality. A well-tended Russian Orthodox church, apparently unused except for Sunday services, is on the corner of 121st Street and Madison Avenue. The other buildings on the block are three- and four-story buildings with only an occasional fire escape showing. In contrast to the obvious wearing away of paint, the prevailing chalk scrawls, and the dented, overflowing garbage cans that characterize the houses south of the school, the residences here reveal attempts to maintain cleanliness and attractiveness. The houses on these blocks are also fronted by a wider expanse of sidewalk which makes for a quieter, less crowded appearance.

The southern boundary line of the school district is 116th Street from Park Avenue to Fifth Avenue. The western cutoff point runs up Fifth Avenue from 116th to 122nd Streets. Much of this western portion of the school's district is taken up by Mt. Morris Park and by Cooper Junior High School. Therefore, the bulk of the school's population comes from south of the school, from 119th to 120th Street between Park and Madison Avenue, and from 116th to 119th Street between Park and Fifth Avenue.

Madison Avenue, which represents the center of the school district, is a heavily traveled street. When children are going to and from school, policemen are stationed at both 119th and 120th Streets on Madison Avenue to aid with safety, even though there are traffic lights on both corners. Although some of their efforts are directed at controlling passing automobiles, the police spend a great deal of time getting children to remain at corners and to cross safely. Many younger children cross the streets either unsupervised or under the supervision of an older sibling. There are also many youngsters who, because of lack of play space, are accustomed to using the streets as play areas. The one park in the district, Mt. Morris Park, has minimal play space. Much of the park is taken up by a steep hill, and what play area is available is usually occupied by older junior high school boys. In addition, parents are often loath to have smaller children go to the park because it sometimes serves as a gathering place for alcoholics and drifters.

Statistics reveal a substantially higher rate of deaths due to motor vehicle accidents among persons under twenty-five in the Harlem area than in the rest of New York City (6.9 per 100,000 compared with 4.2 for all of New York City). Accidents in the

P.S. 79 school district have contributed to these figures. In the immediate vicinity of the school, three different children were hit by automobiles within a year. One of the accidents resulted in the death of a child. There were other frequent reports of children being involved in accidents as they played in the streets on weekends or after school.

The area from 116th to 119th Street is made up primarily of dwellings built before 1930. Interspersed are occasional small business establishments. A clearer picture of the housing situation in the community is given by the 1960 Census of Housing. Of approximately 2,200 dwellings in the neighborhood, almost two-thirds are described as "deteriorating" or "dilapidated." The definitions of these terms by the Census Bureau reveal the low state of housing that exists.

"Deteriorating": needs more repair than would be provided in the course of regular maintenance. It has one or more defects of an immediate nature that must be corrected if the unit is to continue to provide safe and adequate shelter. Examples include holes, open cracks, or missing materials over a small area of the floors, walls, or roof; rotted window sills or frames; deep wear on stairs, floors, or doorsills; broken or loose stair treads or missing balusters.

"Dilapidated": does not provide safe or adequate shelter. Has one or more critical defects; or has a combination of intermediate defects in sufficient number to require extensive repair or rebuilding; or is of inadequate original construction. Critical defects result from continued neglect or indicate serious damage to the structure. Examples include holes, open cracks, or missing materials over a large area of the floors, walls, roof, or other parts of the structure; sagging floors, walls, or roof; damage by storm or fire.

The difficulties caused by the poor housing situation are compounded by overcrowding. The Census Bureau indicates that

What is the community like?

30 per cent of the housing units in the area have one or more persons living in each room. One of the reasons for the apparent overcrowding is that many large families live in the school district. For example, an investigation of the families of the sixth-grade children in the school reveals four families with ten children, five families with nine children, nine families with eight children, and three families with seven children.

As a residential community, then, the community around the school is unsafe, deteriorating, and overcrowded. The implications for the school are many. Inadequate heating and ventilation, and crowded sleeping quarters increase the rate of acute respiratory infections and infectious childhood diseases. Crowded or inadequate kitchens, poor electrical connections, and poorly lighted and unstable stairs accelerate the rate of home accidents. Therefore a strong focus on safety and health education for pupils and parents is necessary. Desirable play areas must be found and their use encouraged.

Teachers who are aware of the housing situation can understand more easily how personal possessions become desperately important to the children who have no bit of space, no piece of property that is solely their own. Perhaps herein lies the reason for the struggles over pencils, desks, and notebook paper.

The low state of living conditions makes an apartment in a housing project something to be fervently desired. This is indicated by the number of parents who say they are trying to move into a project, by the number of applications to housing projects on which the school is asked to comment about the behavior and adjustment of children, and by such comments of children as the following:

"I would like to live in a housing project because I could take hot baths then."

"If I can't live in a castle, I'd like to live in a housing project."

"I like a project because it has grass in front of it."

131

A handbook for teaching in the ghetto school

Unsatisfactory housing makes for a population that is highly transient. This is clearly revealed by the number of children who were admitted and discharged during the school year 1963-64. Of approximately 1,700 total school population, 576 children transferred out of the school during a one-year period. This continuous exodus sometimes results in teachers having children on their registers who are not attending classes. Very often in these cases the child has returned to the South with his family, and the school attendance officer has been unable to trace him.

While 576 children were leaving the school, 763 children were admitted. Included among these were children from the South, children returning to East Harlem after having lived with another part of the family in another area of the city, and an occasional child from another section of the country.

The mobility of the school district's population is further evidenced by the fact that in the census tract that includes P.S. 79's district, of the 8,119 people living there in 1960, more than a third did not live there in 1955.

This constant turnover in pupil population confronts teachers with the problem of dealing with changing groups. It demands not only much more clerical work but an approach in the classroom that helps to orient newcomers to new classmates, a new school, and a new community.

There is a striking imbalance between the number of males and females over fourteen years of age that live in the school district. According to the 1960 Census there were over a thousand more adult females than adult males living in the school neighborhood. This indicates that the school is more likely to have contact with a female representative of a family and also points to a possible reason why many children have expressed the idea that they would like more male teachers in school.

The concern of the children with possessions and with ways of earning money may reflect a school community where the rate of unemployment is much above the national average for both males and females, and where the median family income is $3,500 a year. In addition, further study of family incomes revealed a considerable number of families who earn under $3,000 for the year, a figure designated as the poverty level by the federal government. So it is not astonishing that a survey of P.S. 79's school population showed that 85 per cent of the children come from families on welfare.

Family representatives are frequently asked whether they are on welfare when they apply for accommodations in housing projects, for dental care, for free school lunches, and for psychological help at agencies. Often the school, in its follow-up efforts to ascertain the causes of excessive absence, will be asked to pressure the Department of Welfare to get clothing to a family so that children can get to school. A telephone call to a caseworker often succeeds in speeding up the process of forwarding the expected allotment. Despite this constant exposure of family financial straits, it is not difficult to recognize a sensitivity to being on welfare in some families. This sensitivity is exemplified by a woman who apologetically states: "There's not much I can do. Either I leave the kids home alone when I go to work or stay home with them and get a welfare check."

Another woman says: "I won't have my children see me on welfare. I know too many families where that's all they've learned. Welfare is all they know."

The shame that some families feel about being on welfare is indicated by the observation of one teacher. He described how, as he entered a store in the neighborhood, he saw a parent about to give the storekeeper a welfare check. The parent, noticing the teacher, turned her head and drew in her shoulders as if trying to make herself invisible.

The jobs held by people in the community fall into distinct patterns. Unskilled jobs and service positions are the prevailing

133

occupations. A few of the people are employed as clerks, laborers and craftsmen. Only a miniscule group is in a professional or technical occupation. In view of these facts it can be considered a logical step, if occupational aspirations are to be heightened, to give the children contact with Negro males in professional and technical positions. (Western Electric, Bell Telephone, and other companies will arrange for Negro males holding such positions as engineer, publicist, and personnel interviewer to come talk to the children about their jobs.)

There is probably a direct correlation between the type of occupation held by adult members of the community and the extent of their education. The fact that most of the jobs demand minimal educational requirements is consistent with the statistic that the median of school years completed is 8.3.

A minister in the community described some of the problems caused by parental lack of education in the following way:

> Many of the parents are sensitive about their lack of schooling. They're quick to recognize when they're being patronized, when they're being treated without respect. I've heard of teachers who scold parents as if they were children, and of other teachers who paint only a rosy picture of what happens in the school because they don't think the parents will understand the problems that exist. This isn't treating them with respect. And it's not treating them with respect to give parents only a menial part to play in the education of their children. It's not enough to ask them only to feed and clothe their children properly. They want to be involved in the learning of their children. They want guidance with such things as how they can help their children with reading, where they can take their children on trips, and how they can find out about how their children learn arithmetic. The parents want to feel as though they have a meaningful part to play in the education of their children.

The churches of East Harlem represent an important channel of expression for the community. Such religious leaders as the minister quoted above are spokesmen for the feelings of many of the people in the area. The influence of religion is felt in the school. Although only about five per cent of the schoolchildren participate in the released-time religious instruction provided by the churches, with which the school cooperates, many more attend church and are influenced by religion. They know religious songs. They go to confession. Their concept of morality is affected by a view of an Almighty Being who condemns sin and praises good deeds.

A walk through the neighborhood reveals churches on every block. Their names cross the viewer's eye in quick succession— Mt. Pisgah Baptist Church, Church for All People, The Church of God Gathering, Providence Baptist Church, Apostolic Church, House of God, City of Refuge Church, Ebenezer Baptist Church, and Mt. Lebanon Baptist Church are only some of the churches within a five-block area. The influence of the churches carries over to some of the business establishments in the community. This is evidenced by the names of two of them, the Ontology Restaurant and the Mt. Pisgah Candy Store.

There are some churches outside the immediate school district which are attended by children who go to P.S. 79. There is, for example, the Elmendorf Reformed Church which, in addition to its regular church services, conducts a remedial reading group for children, is a meeting place for a Boy Scout troop and was the setting of a Freedom School during the New York City school boycott.

St. Paul's Roman Catholic Church is also attended by children of the school. In some few cases a child in the public school has a brother or sister going to the parochial school run by St. Paul's. Half of the children who take part in released-time religious instruction attend St. Paul's program.

Indicative of the tenuous foundation of the storefront churches is the fact that two of these church buildings are now boarded up and obviously not in current use.

135

A handbook for teaching in the ghetto school

Boarded-up buildings are not a rarity in the school district. They appear to be part of a deteriorating neighborhood. Ten such buildings were noted during a walk around the school district. In addition, there are five empty lots which serve only as dumping grounds for refuse and junk, and as makeshift playgrounds for children.

The type of business establishment in the community also runs to pattern. There are some small grocery stores but not even one large store of the supermarket variety. (Some of the teachers have had to take their classes as far as 125th Street in order to acquaint them with a supermarket.) There are luncheonettes, sandwich shops, and small restaurants; six beauty shops and three barber shops; only one drug store; a liquor store and many bars. Small businesses are few, and those that exist provide food necessities, deal with physical appearance, or serve drinks. Much of the family shopping, therefore, must be done in the many stores, both large and small, on 125th Street.

New teachers in East Harlem complain that they are unfamiliar with the many community agencies which the children in the school know or should be told about. That many of the children have agency contact is indicated by the fact that during one school year the school guidance counselors referred approximately 180 children to various community agencies. One regular sign of community agency effect on the school occurs every Friday morning when about forty children are taken to the Guggenheim Dental Clinic for treatment.

Teachers frequently must know where to direct children for dental help, where to direct parents whose children are absent from school because they don't have shoes or overcoats, where needed eyeglasses can be obtained, and where children can be sent for supervised recreation.

A beginning acquaintance with the East Harlem community surrounding the school can be obtained by walking through

136

the neighborhood, by going into the stores, by visiting the community centers, and by entering the churches. But a community is more than its physical structures. It is more importantly the people in it; it is what they think and desire and, with particular reference to education, what they expect of the school.

Within the total community there are sub-communities. One such is the community of addicts. Fifth Avenue and 118th Street has been referred to as the corner where more dope passes hands than anywhere else in the world. The occasional break-in that occurs in the school, when typewriters, tape recorders, and television sets are sought as barter for funds, is likely the work of addicts desperate for financial support of their habit. The inhabitants of the community feel that the addicts are a blot on the neighborhood, and their remarks express the desire to be rid of them. Contrary to popular belief, however, the addicts would not seem to be a threat to teachers and children during the school day. This is borne out by the following observation of a teacher:

"Most of these people, when schoolchildren come by, will stand and look at them. I've noticed dope addicts standing on the corner, and when the teacher passes with the class, they try to straighten up, to look their best. They don't want those children to see them in the position that they're in."

There is also the community of people who seek to maintain their sense of personal autonomy, integrity, and capacity for self-direction in the midst of narcotics addiction, dirty streets, and deteriorating housing. These are people who tell you they are searching for an apartment elsewhere in the city, who often exert so tight a hold on the lives of their children that they do not permit them in the streets to play, and who almost compulsively describe the perils of living in the neighborhood.

Another community of people strives to support and supervise large families without the help of a strong male figure.

137

They use older siblings to care for younger children and the household, and they come to school only when deep trouble calls them there. They present to many teachers the picture of apathy. Often they are weary and overburdened, and feel helpless and fearful before school authorities who ask an educational ability they do not possess and a degree of control that they have neither the skill nor the resources to apply.

A parent, active in the school's Parents Association, offered a possible reason for the apparent lack of interest of some parents when she said: "I won't give excuses for people. Parents should come to school to see about their children. But maybe they don't because for so long the Negro people have been promised so much and have been given so little. . . . Someone has the responsibility to find out why parents don't come to school and to do things that will make them want to come to school."

Finally, some people have no hope; they have given up completely. These are people who at one time may have sought work without success and who now see no use in looking any more. These are the men who stand on street corners and the women who stare idly out of windows.

Common to the great majority of people in the community, however, is the belief that education has worth. At parent-teacher-child conferences, parents will frequently be heard remonstrating with their children by saying: "Your teacher has already got her education. Now you've got to get yours. You listen to your teacher."

The groups of unemployed who stand around passing the time give the children and adults daily visible evidence of how a lack of education militates against finding employment. In addition, the community has been flooded with school statements, governmental agency bulletins, and newspaper comments often enough to get the message that education makes for better jobs.

138

What then do the people of the community expect of the school? For one thing, they would like the school to view the community with an unstereotyped eye, to see the diversity that exists. One parent put it this way: "We have many good situations as well as bad ones. We have mothers who try hard with their children and others who don't because they don't know how or don't have the time. We have many families on welfare. Some of them have given up; but there are many mothers on welfare who try to make a good life for their children and who dress them properly even though the welfare money doesn't cover all the clothing needed."

The parents of the community expect that teachers will learn about the neighborhood and the people in it. One parent expressed the feelings of many when she said: "The people of the community resent those teachers who have bad things to say about the community and never come outside the school. The parents say to themselves, 'What do these people know about our community? They just drive to school and drive away. What do they know about us?'" These are parents who find things to be proud of in their community and are angered by the constant disparagement it receives.

Parents ask that teachers reach out to learn about the community. They say: "Teachers should know about the average income of families, that people are poor. They should know that many parents receive A.D.C. [Aid to Dependent Children] because the father is not there, not because they want to. They should know about the crowded conditions, the rats, the people who have to pay a hundred dollars for condemned apartments. They should know we try and we can't get other housing."

The parents go on to suggest: "What we need is someone from the community to work with the parents and the school, someone who knows the people, because the parents are afraid to give their insides to teachers. They will to someone from the community."

139

A handbook for teaching in the ghetto school

The people expect that the school will communicate a faith in the ability of their children to learn. They don't want to hear that their children are disadvantaged or culturally deprived. One parent put it this way: "We are tired of hearing that our children can't learn. They can do as children in other schools do. They need teachers who believe they can."

One of the major sources of some parents' complaints is what they consider a lack of firm discipline in the school. Frequently parents will comment that the school is not tight enough. One parent said it this way: "Children have to be made to obey rules. They'll behave if strict rules are laid down. The school doesn't act strictly enough with children who cause problems."

Basically, then, the parents of the community expect that teachers will recognize the variations in people and families, move into the community with open minds, deal firmly with their classes, show a belief in the ability of the children to learn, and help the children to achieve.

8 What challenges remain?

A teacher equipped with all possible knowledge, experience, maturity, and insight will still find himself faced with challenges that are paradoxical, enigmatic, and frustrating. The words of the people involved with the education of children in the ghetto indicate these challenges.

A leader of a community civil rights group speaks: "Our children are exactly the same as other children. There's absolutely nothing different about them."

A professional educator states: "Many of the children bear the scars of intellectual understimulation in their early years. . . . The language they use may represent a complete lack or distortion of acceptable English."

A minister in the community says: "Our children are great

141

psychologists. They've been 'put on' by so many people that they've learned to get beneath the surface to find the real person."

A teacher gives his idea: "Sure, I could describe them as a group. I could say that they're more likely to be aggressive or defensive. But if when you look at them you see a sea of faces rather than an individual child, you're lost."

The task ahead then is to describe, as fully as possible, the children from the ghetto in terms that can be applied generally, and at the same time to communicate the realization that backgrounds vary and individuals differ. The challenge for the new teacher is to develop generalizations, to apply them judiciously, see their value, and recognize their drawbacks.

It is usually accepted that if a new teacher makes home visits and spends time in the school community, shopping areas, recreational centers, streets, and parks, he will come closer to the real life of his pupils. But the job of the new teacher is to look beyond what he sees. One parent put it this way: "A teacher can walk into an overcrowded apartment and see roaches streaming down a wall and then ask himself, How can people live this way? He can sympathize or he can condemn. What he has to understand is that people don't *want* to live this way, that people aren't *responsible* for these conditions, that they'd like to *change* them but they can't."

Thus the challenge for the new teacher is not only to observe closely but to examine in depth the causes behind what he sees.

A principal tells of a problem in his school: "Many of our children come to school without breakfast. To prepare these children properly for the school day we've established a breakfast club where children are provided with the nutrition necessary for them to be alert."

A teacher describes her children: "So many of them come from homes where nobody cares, where love and affection are

142

totally absent. I try to fill that void for them. I show them that I care."

A militant parent retorts: "All this talk about nutrition and love and affection are excuses for not teaching. Teachers spend their time teaching to the environment rather than to the child. Even if they don't say it, they think to themselves that they can't expect children from such miserable backgrounds to learn much of anything."

The challenge for the new teacher is not only to learn about the child in his environment but to use this knowledge to let each pupil know that he expects a little more than the pupil thinks he can produce. The challenge is to see the problems but not to allow them to stand as insurmountable barriers in the way of learning. The challenge is to create an atmosphere of striving and of progress.

Another challenge is revealed by the parent who says: "How can the school sit calmly by when so many children enter the sixth grade reading second- and third-grade books? How can the principal and teachers sleep at night when they know they've failed in their job of teaching these children to read?" This challenge is reinforced by the remark of the educator who says, "A pupil's learning is, in large measure, a function of the kind of teaching to which he is exposed."

The HARYOU report *Youth in the Ghetto* points out that the results of standardized tests in Harlem elementary schools indicate a rapid deterioration in achievement from grades three to six. It infers from this that the source of educational problems in Harlem elementary schools "lies in the processes which occur during the time they are in school, *rather than in the processes prior to their entrance into school.*"

Some principals and teachers respond in this way: "We do a remarkable job with the children when you consider that many of them don't see books at home, have never been taken any

143

place, and don't have anybody at home who has the time or inclination to ask them about school. They are children who come to school unprepared because they're sleepy, improperly fed, or emotionally disturbed."

The task for the new teacher is not to debate where the fault lies for lack of achievement, but rather to commit himself to the belief that the children *can* learn, to communicate this belief, to develop approaches that will make for pupil learning, and to work toward programs that will compensate for gaps in the necessary background for learning.

A principal comments on how a new teacher should use his time: "I would say that a new teacher needs about two hours each night to plan his daily program adequately."

In *Teaching in the Elementary School,* Herbert Klausmeier, Katherine Dresden, Helen Davis, and Walter Wittich state:

> There are many activities in which the teacher may engage in order to become more effective and improve herself each year she teaches. . . . Participating in in-service educational programs of the school system, taking evening or summer courses in a college, traveling, reading books and journals about the profession, and carrying on experiments in the classroom are types of activities which enable the teacher to improve her efficiency.

A parent says:

> We expect teachers to identify with the community. They're not just visitors from nine to three. We expect them to consider our problems as their problems. If bad housing and narcotics addiction are community problems, then they're the teachers' problems also. If the school is going to be put on short-time session or is lacking the necessary materials or personnel, then we expect teachers to join with us in protesting and not just sit back and watch from the sidelines.

The challenge for the new teacher is to recognize the inter-relationships between the school and the community, to determine the level of personal commitment necessary for doing a successful job of teaching, and to find ways of improving himself as a teacher and working effectively in his position at the same time.

A Negro parent speaking to a white school administrator indicates another problem when she says: "You don't really care whether our children get a decent education. You've gotten yours, and your children will get their education. That's all you care about."

Civil rights groups charge that children in ghetto schools are exposed to teachers who are inferior, who do not expect the children to learn, and who because of their inexperience are ineffective. These charges receive some substantiation from boards of education in both subtle and direct ways. When boards speak about a desire to bring quality education to ghetto schools, it is broadly implied that inferior education is the classroom norm. When teachers with substitute licenses and teachers with little experience make up the majority of faculties in depressed-area elementary schools, the deduction may follow that many classes are exposed to inferior teachers.

Kenneth Clark, in the *New York Times Magazine* in April 1965, wrote: "But whites who try to be free must have the courage to accept the inevitable chaos and confusion of a changing society. There will be inevitable irrationalities in any move to a higher stage of rationality and justice."

The new teacher therefore needs to recognize that as part of a ghetto elementary school faculty he may be characterized as an inferior teacher and as one who lacks concern for the children. The challenge is to develop the inner strength that will permit him to take criticism, much of which may be unwarranted. It is not to withdraw in the face of these attacks but to understand their inception. It is to be aware that in the Negro's struggle to undo past injustice the teacher's role is an ambivalent one, for he represents a different race or a different class, or both. The challenge is to move forward without expecting superhuman responses from himself or from members of the community.

For the new teacher to accept the total challenge is to accept a deep degree of commitment. It is to recognize the need for a growing personal perception. It is to immerse himself in what may be a unique situation, to try to understand the forces working within that situation, and to learn ways of reaching his pupils so that he may truly realize his potential to effect change.

Appendix A. Books for children

All of these books have some relation to the life of the Negro. Books have not been included if, in my view, they are patronizing in tone or lack literary merit. Those listed are books which portray Negro characters, reveal the culture heritage of the Negro, or tell of lives of Negroes who have made significant contributions to the total American culture. I suggest that the teacher not rely totally on this list for the class's literature program but rather incorporate some of these selections along with other samples of good literature when they most appropriately fit into class activities.

AARDEMA, VERNA. *Tales from the Story Hat: African Folk Tales.* New York: Coward-McCann, 1960. Nine tales from Africa, all of which have animals as the main characters. Included are the tricky rabbit, Anansi the spider, and the lion. Many of the stories purport to explain natural phenomena.

147

BEIM, JERROLD. *Swimming Hole.* New York: Morrow, 1950. A picture book that ridicules color prejudice in such a way that the youngest child can understand its point.

BEIM, LORRAINE and JERROLD. *Two Is a Team.* New York: Harcourt, Brace, 1945. Two boys differ on the best way to build a coaster, but after double smash-ups they decide that cooperation makes the most sense. The racial difference of the two children is indicated only by the illustrations.

BISHOP, CLAIRE HUCHET. *Martin de Porres.* Boston: Houghton Mifflin, 1954. Lima, a city of poverty and despair in the early seventeenth century, is the birthplace of this Negro who became doctor, priest, and protector of the poor and unfortunate. The drawings and style of the author make up a moving portrait.

BONTEMPS, ARNA. *Frederick Douglass: Slave-Fighter-Freeman.* New York: Knopf, 1959. The story of an ex-slave who became one of America's foremost fighters against slavery. The author recounts the tale in an interesting, simple manner.

——————. *Lonesome Boy.* Boston: Houghton Mifflin, 1955. A poetically told story of a young boy who follows his love of the trumpet to New Orleans where he has some haunting experiences. Contains mature wisdom.

——————. *Sad-Faced Boy.* Boston: Houghton Mifflin, 1937. Three brothers, one of whom has a sad face which belies a tender, imaginative soul underneath, come to New York to visit their uncle. Here they marvel at a subway ride, a circus parade, and an open-air market. They also become clearly aware of the differences between Harlem and their home in Alabama. An extremely well-written story.

——————. *Story of the Negro.* New York: Knopf, 1960. A concise description of the history of the Negro in Africa and the United States.

CLAYTON, ED. *Martin Luther King.* Englewood Cliffs, N.J.: Prentice-Hall, 1964. This biography written for children tells of the development of Martin Luther King as leader of the non-violent civil rights movement. It describes his roots, his family in which dignity was so important, and his achievements in school. Although brief, the book covers the highlights of his life.

COBB, ALICE. *Swimming Pool.* New York: Friendship Press, 1957. A touching story of how a group of boys band together to build

Appendix A. Books for children

a swimming pool. In the process of working together they succeed in changing the attitudes of the community toward members of different minority groups.

COURLANDER, HAROLD. *Terrapin's Pot of Sense*. New York: Holt, 1957. A varied selection of tales of Negro folklore told as if by a single storyteller. Many end with morals unique for their humor and deep wisdom. Recommended highly.

COURLANDER, HAROLD, and GEORGE HERZOG. *The Cowtail Switch and Other West African Stories*. New York: Holt, 1947. African folk tales which contain talking animals and Anansi, the tricky man-spider. The stories give life to inanimate objects and give explanations of natural phenomena in terms which occasionally reach a poetic level.

COURLANDER, HAROLD, with ALBERT KAFI PREMPEH. *The Hat-Shaking Dance and Other Tales from the Gold Coast*. New York: Harcourt, Brace, 1957. Anansi, the man-spider, is once again the protagonist of these stories which explain natural facts and animal ways. It is interesting to note the similarities with U.S. Negro and West Indian folk tales.

DAVIS, RUSSELL, and BRENT ASHABRANNER. *The Lion's Whiskers: Tales of High Africa*. Boston: Little, Brown, 1959. These are folk stories from Ethiopia which generally show how a tricky, clever protagonist outwits his foes. The stories have been selected from the folklore of the various tribes of Ethiopia.

DEANGELI, MARGUERITE. *Bright April*. New York: Doubleday, 1948. The story of a ten-year-old Negro's beginning acquaintance with prejudice, and how the warmth of her personality helps her to overcome encounters with thoughtlessness. A simply written story which clearly communicates the essence of the main character.

ELTING, MARY, and MARGARET GOSSETT. *Patch*. New York: Doubleday, 1949. This is the story of how a dog helps to save a field of wheat. The major characters are two white boys and a Negro girl. The subject of race is never mentioned.

FAULKNER, GEORGENE. *Melindy's Happy Summer*. New York: Messner, 1949. A young Negro girl joins a farm family as an ambassador of good will. The story tells how she manages to overcome initial personality conflicts and turn her summer into a happy one.

149

A handbook for teaching in the ghetto school

FAULKNER, GEORGENE, and JOHN BECKER. *Melindy's Medal.* New York: Messner, 1945. An eight-year-old girl comes from a family of medal winners. Her grandmother tells her the stories behind these medals, but she cannot hide her disappointment at the fact that the girl, Melindy, is an unlikely medal winner. The book tells of Melindy's school life and of how she, too, wins a medal.

FRITZ, JEAN. *Brady.* New York: Coward-McCann, 1960. Brady Minton grows from a boy who couldn't keep a secret into one who assists his father in transporting slaves in the Underground Railroad.

GARDNER, L. S. *Sal Fisher, Brownie Scout.* New York: Franklin Watts, 1953. A seven-year-old girl joins the Brownie scouts and has various experiences which help her to overcome her awkwardness and to develop her skills. An incidental feature of the book is the fact that two Negro girls are included in the Brownie Troop.

GRAHAM, LORENZ. *North Town.* New York: Crowell, 1965. This is the story of a boy whose family has recently arrived in the North from the South. It describes his struggle for adjustment in a new society, his disappointments, his defensiveness, his relationships with others. Although not as high quality a book as Dorothy Sterling's *Mary Jane,* it can be enjoyed by mature sixth-graders.

HOGAN, INEZ. *Nappy Has a New Friend.* New York: Dutton, 1947. Only the illustrations indicate racial differences in this simple story of friendship.

HOLBROOK, SABRA. *Getting to Know the Virgin Islands, U.S.A.* New York: Coward-McCann, 1959. A report on the Virgin Islands from its past history of pirates and slavers to its present of tourists, year-round sun, and exotic animal life. Purely descriptive but interesting.

HUGHES, LANGSTON. *Famous American Negroes.* New York: Dodd, Mead, 1964. Brief reports on the accomplishments of Negroes in such varied fields as poetry (Phillis Wheatley), business (Charles C. Spaulding), medicine (Daniel Hale Williams), and theater (Ira Aldridge).

——————. *Famous Negro Music Makers.* New York: Dodd, Mead, 1963. Short biographical accounts of Negroes who have contributed to the American musical scene. In addition to telling of such famous Negroes as Marian Anderson, Duke Ellington, and Louis Armstrong, reports on such lesser known Negroes as

150

Dean Dixon, Leadbelly, and James A. Bland are included. Appropriate for older children.

_____. *First Book of Negroes.* New York: Franklin Watts, 1952. Terry, a Negro boy in New York, learns from his family how people of his race have made distinguished contributions to American life.

_____. *The First Book of the West Indies.* New York: Franklin Watts, 1956. The geography, history, and present status of the islands of the West Indies are colorfully described. A brief, simple introduction to the people and land of palm trees, beaches, and sunshine.

HUNT, MABEL LEIGH. *Ladycake Farm.* Philadelphia: Lippincott, 1952. The Freed family moves to a farm to live. The story describes how the children adjust to school and how the antagonism of a neighbor to Negroes is overcome. The most charming part of the book is the description of the family's use of a dictionary as reading matter.

JOHNSON, GYNETH. *How the Donkeys Came to Haiti and Other Tales.* New York: Devin-Adair, 1949. Haitian folk tales that are crammed full of demons and unfrightening monsters. Told in simple terms that are likely to appeal to children. Offers explanations for characteristics of certain animals.

JUSTUS, MAY. *New Boy in School.* New York: Hastings House, 1963. As the only Negro boy in an all-white class, Lennie Lane has feelings of fear and strangeness. He has positive experiences which help him to overcome these feelings. The book, written for younger children, can be used to move into a discussion of how Negro children might feel as members of a minority group in an integrated school.

KEATS, EZRA JACK. *John Henry, An American Legend.* New York: Pantheon, 1965. The story of John Henry is retold with the aid of colorful illustrations. The language is simple but undistinguished.

_____. *The Snowy Day.* New York: Viking, 1962. A picture book which was awarded the Caldecott medal as the most distinguished picture book for children. It is the story of a boy's adventures on a snowy day. The fact that the boy is Negro is incidental to the story. The author presents many charming ideas. For example, at one point, the boy wonders what happened to a snowball he put in his pocket.

151

——————. *Whistle for Willie.* New York: Viking, 1964. Little Peter wanted terribly to learn how to whistle for his dog just as big boys did. With beautiful illustrations the author takes us along with Peter for a day as he pursues the secret of learning how to whistle.

KENWORTHY, LEONARD S. *Profile of Nigeria.* New York: Doubleday, 1960. The author concisely and lucidly describes the contrasts that make up Nigeria. The material is organized around such topics as history, clothing, health, people, food, and arts and crafts.

LANG, DON. *On the Dark of the Moon.* New York: Oxford, 1952. This is the story of how a boy befriends and tames two raccoons. The characterizations of the boy and his unusual pets are delightfully and clearly drawn. Might be a familiar setting for children who know southern rural life.

LEVY, MIMI COOPER. *Corrie and the Yankees.* New York: Viking, 1959. Corrie, a ten-year-old Negro girl whose father is a scout for the Union forces, becomes a heroine herself when she hides and cares for a wounded Yankee soldier.

LEWIS, RICHARD. *Summer Adventure.* New York: Harper and Row, 1962. Ross Pennock uses his summer to develop a zoo from animals he has discovered and captured at a nearby quarry. The only indications that Ross is Negro are the book cover picture and the story illustrations.

LEXAU, JOAN M. *Benjie.* New York: Dial, 1964. A delightful story of a very bashful boy and his grandmother. Benjie was so shy that he wouldn't talk to anybody. But one day he searches for his grandmother's precious lost earring and in the process conquers his shyness.

LINCOLN, C. ERIC. *The Negro Pilgrimage in America.* New York: Bantam, 1967. Designed as supplementary classroom material, this book describes the contributions, history, and heritage of American Negroes from 1600 to the present. Includes capsule biographies of those who have made noteworthy accomplishments. Profusely illustrated, the book contains an easy-reference chronology of important events.

MARTIN, PATRICIA MILES. *Little Brown Hen.* New York: Crowell, 1960. The disappearance of Willie's little brown hen and his search for two little ducks for his mother's birthday make up this tale with its country setting. The fact that the story has all Negro characters is revealed only by the illustrations.

RANDALL, BLOSSOM. *Fun for Chris*. Chicago: Whitman, 1956. This is the story of a little boy's friendship with a Negro boy and his curiosity about the difference in skin color. A brief, simple answer is given to Chris's questions about race.

RICKERT, EDITH. *The Bajabi Tree*. New York: Doubleday, 1940. A simple adaptation of an African folk tale in which a tortoise outdoes other animals in remembering the name of a tree. The author makes great use of repetition as a technique in her telling of the story.

ROLLINS, CHARLEMAE. *Christmas Gif'*. Chicago: Follett, 1963. An anthology of Christmas poems, songs, and stories written by and about Negroes. Contains some real gems.

SCHLOAT, G. WARREN, JR. *Kwaku, A Boy of Ghana*. New York: Knopf, 1962. Using bright photographs and simple text the author gives views of the life of a boy in modern Ghana. The book can be valuable as a way of dissipating stereotypes about African children and of showing the similarities to the lives of boys and girls in New York.

SHERLOCK, PHILIP M. *Anansi, the Spider Man: Jamaican Folk Tales*. New York: Crowell, 1954. These tales of a man who also was a spider are African in origin. Anansi's trickery and guile result in stories whose innocence, humor, gaiety, and simplicity are likely to appeal to children.

SHOTWELL, LOUISA R. *Roosevelt Grady*. New York: World, 1963. This tale of a Negro migrant family and the desire of mother and son to find roots and a place where steady schooling is available, succeeds in portraying real characters who have depth of personality.

STERLING, DOROTHY. *Mary Jane*. New York: Doubleday, 1959. A realistic story of the trials of a Negro girl who becomes the first of her race to attend an all-white school. With the current emphasis on school integration, it is an excellent story to use as a take-off point for discussion of the possible problems that may face children in an integrated school.

STEVENSON, AUGUSTA. *George Carver, Boy Scientist*. Indianapolis: Morrill, 1959. The struggle of a boy to achieve his education is recounted in simple terms. His intense interest in plants is described. A straightforward account.

SUTHERLAND, EFUA. *Playtime in Africa.* London: Brown, Knight, and Truscott, 1962. With large photographs and limited text, the similarity of games of African children with those of American children is shown.

SWIFT, HILDEGARDE HOYT. *North Star Shining.* New York: Morrow, 1947. In poetic form and accompanied by brightly colored pictures, this is a brief history of the American Negro.

TARRY, ELLEN, and MARIE HALL ETS. *My Dog Rinty.* New York: Viking, 1946. The photographs of Alexander and Alexandra Alland contribute an air of authenticity to this book about a boy and his troublesome dog. Rinty's penchant for chewing rugs and carpets becomes a virtue when it is discovered that he is gifted at finding mice holes. Language is simple. Plot development is uncomplicated and somewhat superficial.

WEISS, EDNA S. *Truly Elizabeth.* Boston: Houghton Mifflin, 1957. A country girl comes to live in the city, and her friendliness and imagination make for some problems of adjustment in an indifferent metropolis. Her best friends are a girl who happens to be Jewish, and a boy who is Negro. The story climaxes with a successful search for a place to live. A charming, well-told story of children whose religious and racial differences are handled in a natural manner.

WEISS, HARVEY. *Horse in No Hurry.* New York: Putnam, 1961. Paul and John-Thomas involve Herman, a very tired horse, in a race with Jessica and her flea-ridden dog, Morton. The race carries the children into amusing adventures with advertising and police enforcement. The fact that John-Thomas is Negro is incidental to the story.

—————————. *Paul's Horse Herman.* New York: Putnam, 1958. An old, tired horse becomes the property of Paul. With some difficulty he succeeds in getting the horse to move out of his lethargy and to carry his friends, Jessica and John-Thomas, into some interesting adventures.

WHITE, ANNE TERRY. *George Washington Carver.* New York: Random House, 1953. The story of the life of a great Negro scientist, concentrating on his contributions to southern agriculture through discoveries regarding the uses of the peanut and sweet potato. A well-written account that gives a feeling of the character of the man.

WILL and NICOLAS. *Four-Leaf Clover*. New York: Harcourt, Brace, 1959. Two boys search for a four-leaf clover to bring them luck. They find, in addition to the clover, adventures with an angry bull and a runaway horse. Race has nothing to do with this story in which one of the boys is Negro and the other white. Written for younger children.

WOODSON, CARTER GOODWIN. *African Myths*. Washington, D.C.: Associated Publishers, 1948. A collection of folk tales and proverbs from different parts of Africa. Explanations of such things as why dogs live with men and how death came into the world are given in the short stories in which animals are the predominant characters.

WOODY, REGINA. *Almena's Dogs*. New York: Farrar, Straus, 1954. This book tells of a little girl's deep understanding and love of dogs. An interesting sidelight to the story is that Almena, the little girl, is a Negro.

WRISTON, HILDRETH. *Susan's Secret*. New York: Farrar, Straus, 1957. Susan's family is concerned with a secret that leads to night whisperings, the click of harnessware in the dark, and a hidden room. Circumstances involve Susan as a conductor in the underground railway of pre-Civil War days.

YATES, ELIZABETH. *Amos Fortune: Free Man*. New York: Dutton, 1950. A young African prince is captured and brought to America as a slave. He receives good treatment but continues to cherish the idea of his freedom. Once free he devotes his life to bringing liberty to others. The story is rather a tale of a strong personality than a story of slavery.

Appendix B. Books for teachers

The following annotated list of books contains poetry, history, fiction, and factual material which can be helpful in introducing teachers to the feelings, history, cultural background, and present status of children in ghetto elementary schools.

ADAMS, RUSSELL L. *Great Negroes Past and Present*. Chicago: Afro-American, 1964. Brief biographical sketches of Negroes from all parts of the world and all periods of history.

ALLPORT, GORDON W. *ABC's of Scapegoating*. Third revised edition. New York: Anti-Defamation League of B'nai B'rith, 1959. In simple, interesting terms the author describes the mechanics of scapegoating. He briefly indicates the reasons for scapegoating, the sources of race prejudice in children, the forms of scapegoating, and the possible responses of victims.

BARRON, MILTON L., ed. *American Minorities: A Textbook of Readings in Intergroup Relations*. New York: Knopf, 1957. A major section deals with the role of the Negro in American society and the roots of prejudice and discrimination.

Appendix B. Books for teachers

BOOKER, SIMEON. *Black Man's America*. Englewood Cliffs, N.J.: Prentice-Hall, 1964. Using a journalistic style, the author, a Negro reporter, describes various aspects of the Negro's fight for equality. Particularly interesting are his personal views of the attitudes of highly placed government leaders, including the late President Kennedy, of his experience as witness to a clash between Negro and white youths following a football game, and of the influence of various Negro civil rights leaders.

BROOKS, GWENDOLYN. *The Bean Eaters*. New York: Harper, 1960. The works included in this book are a combination of the author's racial experience and a high-quality talent. Particularly powerful are the poems "Bronzeville Woman in a Red Hat," a description of the reaction to a newly hired Negro maid, and "The Ballad of Rudolph Reed," the tragic story of a Negro's search for a home for his family.

BUCKMASTER, HENRIETTA. *Flight to Freedom*. New York: Crowell, 1958. Although much of this book is concerned with the heroism of people involved with the Underground Railroad, more than a little attention is given to the strife that existed between abolitionists and pro-slavery factions. The author, in simple terms, gives the background of the legislation, the social and economic forces, and the personalities involved in the war against slavery. The book can be read by bright sixth-graders.

CLARK, KENNETH B. *Prejudice and Your Child*. Second edition enlarged. Boston: Beacon, 1963. This book discusses the inception of prejudice in children, its detrimental effects on both white and Negro children, and what schools, social agencies, and churches can do to develop structures which utilize human resources more productively. Possibly most pertinent for the teacher is the section which reveals how schools, through subtle measures, reinforce society's patterns of discrimination.

CONANT, JAMES BRYANT. *Slums and Suburbs*. New York: McGraw-Hill, 1961. A well-publicized book which compares slum schools with those in the suburbs. Some of the problems of teachers in low socioeconomic schools are described. The author recommends higher pay as a way to attract higher-quality staff to slum schools. He also makes a strong plea for vocational programs tailored to the vocational aims of students.

DOUGLASS, FREDERICK. *Narrative of the Life of Frederick Douglass, An American Slave*. Cambridge, Mass.: Belknap Press of Harvard

157

University Press, 1960. Dark, painful memories of slavery are recounted in a clear, simple, and effective manner. The horrors of the institution are starkly portrayed in this story of one of the greats of Negro history.

DuBois, William Edward Burghardt. *The Souls of Black Folk.* New York: Avon, 1965. This book, written in 1903, expresses in a surprisingly up-to-date way the plight of the Negro in America. In literate terms it gives explanations for the lack of family stability and the purported high crime rate among Negroes. The author attempts to describe the feelings of Negroes who at the time were less than fifty years out of slavery. One especially moving chapter tells of the differences in the lives of two men brought up on the same plantation, one a Negro and the other white. In every way this is a very modern book.

Ginzburg, Eli. *The Negro Potential.* New York: Columbia University Press, 1956. The author, through the liberal use of statistical tables, portrays the economic and educational status of the Negro in America. The figures he presents show the terrific waste of manpower that results from the lower state of Negroes as compared with whites. The author illustrates the potential of the Negro in an integrated society when he describes the achievements of the Negro soldier in an integrated army in Korea.

Gunther, John. *Meet the Congo and Its Neighbors.* New York: Harper, 1959. Although a little outdated by the rush of political events, the book gives a picture of the African countries of the Congo, Uganda, Tanganyika, the Sudan, and the Cameroons. Without going into great depth, the author describes the history, customs, politics, and educational systems of these countries. The simplicity of style makes this book appropriate for bright sixth-graders.

Harrington, Michael. *The Other America.* New York: Macmillan, 1964. The author describes in sadly vivid terms the poverty that exists for forty to fifty million people in the midst of our "affluent society." One chapter is devoted to poverty in the black ghetto of Harlem. Personal insights are given into what it means to be poor in Harlem.

Hughes, Langston, ed. *An African Treasury.* New York: Crown, 1960. Native black Africans present the problems, the feelings, the personality of Africa through articles, essays, stories, and poems selected by Langston Hughes. Included are samples of the work

158

of such well-known Africans as Tom Mboya, Kwame Nkrumah, and Leopold Sedar Senghor.

—————————. *New Negro Poets: U.S.A.* Bloomington: Indiana University Press, 1965. A wide variety of verse, from descriptive poetry to poetry of protest, of thirty-seven postwar poets.

—————————. *Selected Poems of Langston Hughes.* New York: Knopf, 1959. This is a collection of poems about a variety of topics. Included are such poems as "Afro-American Fragments," "Shadow of the Blues," "Madam to You," and "Words Like Freedom." They are crammed full of genuine feelings that have grown out of the life of the Negro.

HUXLEY, ELSPETH. *A New Earth.* New York: Morrow, 1960. This is a description of a land in the midst of revolutionary change. The author indicates in detail how Kenya's countryside is being transformed by irrigation schemes and settlement experiments. It is interesting to note how progress represents a mixed blessing in that some of the beneficial aspects of the long-ingrained social order are discarded as radical changes are introduced. The problems are a result of a country or society in a rapid flux.

JOHNSON, JAMES WELDON, ed. *The Book of American Negro Poetry.* New York: Harcourt, Brace, 1931. An anthology of the poetic achievement of the American Negro. Representative poems of such poets as Dunbar, Johnson, McKay, Cullen, and Hughes are included.

KATZ, WILLIAM LOREN. *Teachers' Guide to American Negro History.* Chicago: Quadrangle, 1968. This excellent handbook for teachers contains programmatic techniques, resources, and bibliographic and audio-visual references on the Negro. The material is keyed to typical textbook topics and geared for use in the social studies curriculum in junior and senior high schools. The book also contains lists of libraries and museums which house special collections on the Negro.

—————————. *Eyewitness: The Negro in American History.* New York: Pitman, 1967. A comprehensive and fully illustrated American Negro history which follows the traditional courses of study in United States history. It contains many eyewitness accounts never before published as well as information on Negro inventors, cowboys, cultural figures, and reformers not readily available. Useful as a classroom tool for both teachers and students, particularly in secondary schools.

KIRK, SAMUEL. *Educating Exceptional Children*. Boston: Houghton, Mifflin, 1962. This book includes a chapter which describes the typical behavioral deviations of children. There is also a section indicating the characteristics of lower-class children.

LINCOLN, C. ERIC. *The Black Muslims in America*. Boston: Beacon, 1961. This book reviews the activities, beliefs, and goals of Black Islam. The author describes the aspects of American society which have contributed to the origin and development of such protest groups as the Black Muslims.

MCWILLIAMS, CAREY. *Brothers Under the Skin*. Revised edition. Boston: Little, Brown, 1964. A new introduction for this book, originally written in 1943, traces the effect of current happenings on the battle to achieve equal rights for minority groups. In addition to discussing the plight of such minority groups as the Chinese, the Mexicans, the Japanese, and the Puerto Ricans, the author devotes a chapter to the historic development of slavery in the United States, which he sees primarily as a result of economic factors, and the subsequent discrimination against Negroes.

MELTZER, MILTON, ed. *In Their Own Words: A History of the American Negro, 1619-1895*. New York: Crowell, 1964. This book, compiled from letters, newspapers, other books, and journals, tells of the grief and pain of slavery as described by its victims.

NEW YORK CITY BOARD OF EDUCATION. *The Negro in American History*. Board of Education of the City of New York, Curriculum Bulletin No. 4, 1964-65 Series. A broad, factual description of the life of the Negro in American history. The material moves from the African heritage of the Negro and slave days through the Civil War and Reconstruction to the present.

——————. *Call Them Heroes, Book I and Book II*. Morristown, N.J.: Silver Burdett, 1965. Brief biographies of minority-group members who have succeeded in leading productive lives despite the obstacles of poverty, prejudice, or language. The lives of such people in positions as policemen, lawyer, priest, and typesetter are presented.

PETTIGREW, THOMAS F. *A Profile of the Negro American*. Princeton, N.J.: Van Nostrand, 1964. This is a comprehensive survey of research which presents a view of the Negro American, his personality, his genetic composition, his mental and physical health, his intelligence, his crime rate, and his current protest. It can help the teacher who seeks data to counteract many of the

160

popular myths, fallacies, and prejudices concerning the American Negro.

POWLEDGE, FRED. *To Change a Child: A Report on the Institute for Developmental Studies.* Chicago: Quadrangle, 1968. This work focuses on the findings of the Institute directed by Martin Deutsch. It describes the Institute's work with the disadvantaged child— particularly those practical approaches that are attracting a continually growing body of educators—and outlines the Institute's program of "intervention" into the slum child's early life.

REDDING, SAUNDERS. *The Lonesome Road.* New York: Doubleday, 1958. This book describes the Negro's past in America by telling of such famous Negroes as Frederick Douglass, Daniel Hale Williams (surgeon), Thurgood Marshall (attorney), and Robert Abbott (publisher of the *Chicago Defender*). Also indicated are the contributions Negroes have made in helping America to fight its wars.

ROLLINS, CHARLEMAE. *Famous American Negro Poets.* New York: Dodd, Mead, 1965. The author presents biographies of twelve Negro poets who have particular appeal for young people, with brief samples of their work. This book might be enjoyed by bright sixth-graders but is mostly for teachers.

ROTH, HENRY. *Call It Sleep.* New York: Avon, 1965. This is a beautifully written account of the feelings and experiences of an immigrant boy in the slum jungles of the city. The character of the mother is especially delicate and human. The feelings of strangeness and the beauty of inner life that are portrayed can help the teacher to imagine a little of what life in Harlem is like for people whose original surroundings were totally different.

SHAFTEL, GEORGE, and FANNIE R. *Role-Playing the Problem Story.* New York: National Conference of Christians and Jews, 1962. This is a discussion of the techniques of role-playing. It describes such techniques as "warming up the group," preparing the audience, selecting participants, and discussing and evaluating the role-playing. It goes on to present sample problem stories which may be used to assist with the understanding of developmental tasks. One story illustrates the use of role-playing in a program of intergroup education.

SILBERMAN, CHARLES E. *Crisis in Black and White.* New York: Random House, 1964. A well-written analysis of the Negro problem which describes such aspects of the situation as its history, the anger involved, the problem of Negro identification, and the civil rights movement. The author makes pertinent comments regarding the education of the Negro as he refers to pre-kindergarten programs, basal readers planned for Negro children, and the question of immediate school integration.

STEWART, MAXWELL S. *The Negro in America*. New York: Public Affairs Committee, Pamphlet No. 95, 1944. This pamphlet summarizes Myrdal's *An American Dilemma*. It describes the paradox of a society whose ethic is dedicated to equal rights being beset by patterns of discrimination against the Negro. It portrays the status of the Negro in America in 1940 through reference to representation in the professions, to segregation practices, to educational opportunities for the Negro, and to forms of Negro protest. Although somewhat outdated, the pamphlet discusses some of the problems that are still with us.

TRAGER, H. G., and M. R. YARROW. *They Learn What They Live*. New York: Harper, 1952. This is a report of an experiment in intergroup education. The authors indicate how they undertook a program of teacher education and followed it up with a club program in intergroup learning. The book carefully presents the precautions taken to control the variables involved in the experiment, and contains many concrete illustrations of class activities which were designed to modify the attitudes of children.

WAKIN, EDWARD. *At the Edge of Harlem*. New York: Morrow, 1965. With the aid of photographs this book illustrates the life of a middle-class Negro—a teacher in this case—and his family in the Harlem ghetto. A reading of the book can serve to remind the teacher that in his class may be a few middle-class children whose values, home environments, and norms of behavior are different from the lower-class children who comprise the majority of his class. The worth of some of the values portrayed may be open to question.

WEINBERG, MEYER, ed. *Learning Together: A Book on Integrated Education*. Chicago: Integrated Education Associates, 1964. A variety of articles relating in some way to integrated education has been grouped together to give a broad picture of the problems involved in this area. Included are articles which discuss the historical aspects of the question, the effects of segregation on the schooling of children, approaches in teaching children from underprivileged areas, and the legal and political sides of the problem.

162

Bibliography

BOOKS

ASHTON-WARNER, SYLVIA. *Teacher.* New York: Simon and Schuster, 1963.

BALDWIN, JAMES. *The Fire Next Time.* New York: Dial, 1963.

BOSSARD, JAMES H. S., and ELEANOR STOKER BALL. *The Sociology of Child Development.* New York: Harper, 1960.

BRAITHWAITE, E. R. *To Sir, With Love.* London: Bodley Head, 1959.

BROWN, JAMES W., RICHARD B. LEWIS and FRED F. HARCLEROAD, *A-V Instruction Materials and Methods.* New York: McGraw-Hill, 1959.

BUHLER, CHARLOTTE, FAITH SMITTER, SYBIL RICHARDSON and FRANKLYN BRADSHAW. *Childhood Problems and the Teacher.* New York: Holt, 1952.

CROSBY, MURIEL. *An Adventure in Human Relations: A Three-Year Experimental Project on Schools in Changing Neighborhoods, Progress Report, Section I, First Year, 1959-1960; Second Year,*

A handbook for teaching in the ghetto school

1960-1961; Third Year, 1961-1962. Wilmington, Del.: Wilmington Board of Education and the National Conference of Christians and Jews, 1960-63.

DAVIS, ALLISON, and JOHN DOLLARD. *Children of Bondage.* Washington, D.C.: American Council on Education, 1940.

FRAZIER, EDWARD FRANKLIN. *The Negro Family in the United States.* New York: Dryden, 1948.

GILLHAM, HELEN. *Helping Children Accept Themselves and Others.* New York: Bureau of Publications, Teachers College, Columbia University, 1959.

HANDLIN, OSCAR. *The Newcomers: Negroes and Puerto Ricans in a Changing Metropolis.* Cambridge, Mass.: Harvard University Press, 1959.

HARING, NORRIS G., and E. LAKIN PHILLIPS. *Educating Emotionally Disturbed Children.* New York: McGraw-Hill, 1962.

HARYOU Report. *Youth in the Ghetto.* New York, 1964.

KENWORTHY, LEONARD S. *Introducing Children to the World.* New York: Harper, 1956.

KLAUSMEIER, HERBERT J., and others. *Teaching in the Elementary School.* New York: Harper, 1956.

KORNBERG, LEONARD. *A Class for Disturbed Children.* New York: Bureau of Publications, Teachers College, Columbia University, 1955.

LINDSEY, MARGARET, and WILLIAM T. GRUHN. *Student Teaching in the Elementary School.* New York: Ronald, 1957.

MAGARY, JAMES F., and JOHN R. EICHORN, eds. *The Exceptional Child: A Book of Readings.* New York: Holt, Rinehart, and Winston, 1960.

MCGEOCH, DOROTHY M., and others. *Learning to Teach in Urban Schools.* New York: Teachers College Press, Teachers College, Columbia University, 1965.

MIEL, ALICE, and PEGGY BROGAN. *More Than Social Studies.* Englewood Cliffs, N.J.: Prentice-Hall, 1957.

MYRDAL, GUNNAR. *An American Dilemma.* Rev. ed., New York: Harper, 1962.

NEW YORK CITY BOARD OF EDUCATION. *Guide for Newly Appointed Teachers in the New York City Elementary Schools.* Elementary Division, Board of Education of the City of New York, January 1964.

Bibliography

OTTLEY, ROI. *Black Odyssey.* New York: Scribner's, 1950.

PASSOW, A. HARRY, ed. *Education in Depressed Areas.* New York: Bureau of Publications, Teachers College, Columbia University, 1962.

REDL, FRITZ, and DAVID WINEMAN. *Controls From Within.* Glencoe, Ill.: Free Press, 1952.

REDL, FRITZ, and WILLIAM WATTENBERG. *Mental Hygiene in Teaching.* New York: Harcourt, Brace, 1951.

RIESE, HERTHA. *Heal the Hurt Child.* Chicago: University of Chicago Press, 1962.

RIESSMAN, FRANK. *The Culturally Deprived Child.* New York: Harper and Row, 1962.

ROSWELL, FLORENCE, and GLADYS NATCHEZ. *Reading Disability, Diagnosis and Treatment.* New York: Basic Books, 1964.

SENIOR, CLARENCE. *The Puerto Ricans: Strangers—Then Neighbors.* Chicago: Quadrangle, 1965.

SIMPSON, GEORGE EATON. *Racial and Cultural Minorities.* New York: Harper, 1953.

WAKEFIELD, DAN. *Island in the City.* Boston: Houghton Mifflin, 1959.

WASHBURN, RUTH WENDELL. *Children Have Their Reasons.* New York: Appleton-Century-Crofts, 1942.

PERIODICALS

ASBELL, BERNARD. "Not Like Other Children," *Redbook,* October 1963.

BETTELHEIM, BRUNO. "Teaching the Disadvantaged," *NEA Journal,* 54:8-12, September 1965.

BOYD, GEORGE FELIX. "The Levels of Aspiration of White and Negro Children in a Non-Segregated Elementary School," *Journal of Social Psychology,* 36:191-96, 1952.

BRICE, EDWARD WARNER. "Studying Africa," *Childhood Education,* 38:156-58, December 1961.

CROSBY, MURIEL. "Children in Crowded Areas," *Childhood Education,* 39:411-12, May 1963.

DEUTSCH, MARTIN. "Early Social Environment and School Adaptation," *Teachers College Record,* 66:699-706, May 1965.

A handbook for teaching in the ghetto school

_____. "The Role of Social Class in Language Development and Cognition," Institute for Developmental Studies, Department of Psychiatry, New York Medical College, Revised Version of a Paper Read at the Annual Meeting of the American Orthopsychiatric Association, April 1964.

_____. "Social and Psychological Perspectives for the Facilitation of the Pre-School Child," Institute for Developmental Studies, Department of Psychiatry, New York Medical College, Prepared for the Arden House Conference on Pre-School Enrichment of Socially Disadvantaged Children, December 16, 17, and 18, 1962.

DEUTSCH, MARTIN, and BERT BROWN. "Social Influences in Negro-White Intelligence Differences," *Journal of Social Issues*, XX, No. 2, April 1964.

EDGAR, ROBERT, and HELEN STOREN. *Learning to Teach in Difficult Schools*. Flushing, N.Y.: Department of Education, Queens College, March 1963.

EDUCATIONAL POLICIES COMMISSION. *Education and the Disadvantaged American*. Washington, D.C.: National Education Association of the United States, 1962.

ELLIS, RICHARD R. "The Facilitation of Learning for Environmentally Impoverished Children: Implications from Research," Institute for Developmental Studies, Department of Psychiatry, New York Medical College, Presented to Community Action for Youth, Cleveland, Ohio, May 1964.

FISHER, ROBERT J. "Who Is This Lower-Class Child?" *Journal of Educational Sociology*, 34:309-11, March 1961.

FRIEDMAN, MURRAY. "Some Aspects of Cultural Deprivation," *Pathways in Child Guidance*, Board of Education of the City of New York, XIV, No. 4, June 1962.

GOLDBERG, MIRIAM L. "Adapting Teacher Styles to Pupil Differences: Teachers for Disadvantaged Children," *Merrill-Palmer Quarterly of Behavior and Development*, 10,(2): 161-78, April 1964.

HARBURGER, GLADYS, and FLORA BELLE ZALUSKIN. "The Panel of Americans: A Technique for Intergroup Education," *Strengthening Democracy*, Board of Education of the City of New York, XVI, No. 2, January 1964.

HAUBRICH, VERNON F. "The Culturally Disadvantaged and Teacher Education," *The Reading Teacher*, 18:499-505, March 1965.

166

HEIL, LOUIS M. "Personality Variables," *Theory Into Practice*, 3:15, February 1964.

HEIL, LOUIS M., and CARLETON WASHBURNE. "Brooklyn College Research in Teacher Effectiveness," *Journal of Educational Research*, 55:347-51, May 1962.

JOHN, VERA P. "The Intellectual Development of Slum Children: Some Preliminary Findings," *American Journal of Orthopsychiatry*, 33:813-22, 1963.

KELLER, SUZANNE. "The Social World of the Urban Slum Child: Some Early Findings," *American Journal of Orthopsychiatry*, 33,(5):823-31, 1963.

KLINEBERG, OTTO. "Life Is Fun in a Smiling, Fair-Skinned World," *Saturday Review*, February 16, 1963.

LANDOWNE, ALLEN. "Audio-Visual Implications Drawn from Research on the Disadvantaged Child," *A-V Learning*, Board of Education of the City of New York, VIII, No. 2, December-January 1965.

LEVINE, NAOMI, and WILL MASLOW. *A Program for Integrating New York City's Schools*. New York: American Jewish Congress, 1964.

MITCHELL, CHARLES. "The Culturally Deprived—A Matter of Concern," *Childhood Education*, 38:412-20, May 1962.

MORELAND, KENNETH J. "Educational and Occupational Aspirations of Mill and Town School Children in a Southern Community," *Social Forces*, 39:169-75, December 1960.

NEW YORK CITY BOARD OF EDUCATION. *Bridges to Understanding*. Human Relations Unit, Board of Education of the City of New York, 1965.

—————. "The Integration Movement and Education," *Curriculum and Materials*, XVIII, No. 3, Spring 1964.

—————. *Resource Materials on the Effects of Smoking*, 1962.

—————. *What Secondary Schools Can Do About Teenage Narcotics Addiction*, Series No. 3, 1956-67.

RASMUSSEN, MARGARET, ed. *When Children Move from School to School*. Washington, D.C.: Association for Childhood Education, 1960.

RIVLIN, HARRY N. "New Teachers for New Immigrants," *Teachers College Record*, 66:707-18, May 1965.

—————. "Teachers for Our Urban Classrooms," *City College Alumnus*, 58:11-14, January 1962.

167

A handbook for teaching in the ghetto school

SARVIS, MARY A. "Reactions of Children from Crowded Areas," *Childhood Education*, 39:413-15, May 1963.

SLOTKIN, AARON N. "The Treatment of Minorities in Textbooks: The Issues and the Outlook," *Strengthening Democracy*, XVI, No. 3, May 1964.

STULL, EDITH G. "Reading Materials for the Disadvantaged," *Reading Teacher*, 17 (7):522-26, April 1964.

WEINSTEIN, GERALD, and MARIO FANTINI. " 'Phony' Literature," *English Journal*, 54:259-64, April 1965.

WEISSKOPF-JOELSON, EDITH. "Kinds of Intelligence Differ, Too," *NEA Journal*, 44:420-21, October 1955.

WILKINSON, FRANCES R., and RALPH H. OJEMANN. "The Effect on Pupil Growth of an Increase in Teacher Understanding of Pupil Behavior," *Journal of Experimental Education*, 8:143-47, December 1939.

Index

Abstract symbols vs. concrete objects, 115, 122-123
Achievement, deterioration in, during school years, 143
Amsterdam News, 23
Ashton-Warner, Sylvia, 18, 86
Attucks, Crispus, 99
Atypical occurrences, 24-25
Audio-visual materials, 112-114

"Baby" (Hughes), 98
Baldwin, James, 21, 23, 113
Blackboard Jungle, 23
Boots and His Brothers, 87
Braithwaite, E. R., 18
Brown, Claude, 23

Index

Challenge posed by ghetto schools, 16-20, 141-146
Change, children's fears of, 92-94
Children, depressed-area:
    academic deficiencies of, 81-88
    characteristics of, 67-70
    and city agencies, 105-109
    and civil rights activities, 102-105
    curiosity of, 90-92
    experiences of, 72-78, 91
    feelings of, 92-101, 121
    interests of, 78-81, 90-91
    language of, 84-86
    mobility of, 132
    responsibilities of, 68, 74, 76
    restricted contacts of, 109-114
    strengths of, 89-92, 123
    views of, regarding effective and ineffective teaching, 59-67
    See also Misbehavior.
Children of Bondage (Davis and Dollard), 27
City agencies, teaching about operations of, 105-109
Civil rights activities, dealing with, 102-105
Clark, Kenneth, 145
Class for Disturbed Children (Kornberg), 27-28
Classroom:
    decoration of, 28-30, 120-121
    need for organization in, *see* Organization; Routine; Structure.
Clay, Cassius, 98
Controls from Within (Redl and Wineman), 25
Cooper Junior High School, New York City, 128, 129
Craft materials, 124
"Creation, The" (Johnson), 83, 118
Crow Boy (Yashima), 94
Cullen, Countee, 99
Culturally Deprived Child, The (Riessman), 62
Curriculum, development of:
    and city agencies, 105-109

Curriculum, development of *(cont.)*
    and civil rights activities, 102-105
    and non-ghetto contacts, 109-114
    use of children's curiosity in, 90-92, 123
    use of children's experiences in, 71-78, 91
    use of children's feelings in, 92-101, 121
    use of children's interests in, 78-81, 90-91
    use of children's strengths in, 89-92, 123
    use of common academic deficiencies in, 81-88

Davis, Allison, 27
Davis, Helen, 144
Davis, Ossie, 113
Death rate, motor-vehicle, in Harlem, 129
Defiance, 33
Deficiencies, common academic, 81-88
Deutsch, Martin, 82
Displays, classroom, 28-30
    children's contributions to, 30
Dollard, John, 27
Douglass, Frederick, 80, 99
Dramatization materials, 125
Dresden, Katherine, 144
Dumas, Alexander, 100
Dunbar, Paul Laurence, 85, 98, 118, 125

Ebony, 23, 121
Education, value commonly placed on, in ghetto, 138
"Ennui" (Hughes), 118
Enthusiasm, communication of, 44-45
"Esthete in Harlem" (Hughes), 20
Exceptional Child, The (Harper and Wright), 32
Exchange visits, between Negro and white classes, 69
Expectation patterns:
    in children, 26-27
    in teachers, 22-25

Index

Experience charts, 124-125

Failure:
  children's, dealing with, 30-32
  teachers', actions that lead to, 61-62, 64-67
Farmer, James, 113
Fighting, 33-35
Filmstrips, 119-120
Flexibility, need for, 47
Frazier, Edward Franklin, 23
Freedomways, 23
Fromm, Erich, 18

Games and puzzles, 123
Ghetto community, characteristics of. *See* P.S. 79 school district.
Gratification, sources of, in ghetto teaching, 20-21
Guggenheim Dental Clinic, 136

Handlin, Oscar, 23
Harper, Louis, 32
Heil, Louis, 25-26
History, teaching of, 80
  Negro, 97-101
Housing, ghetto, 127-131
Hughes, Langston, 20, 98, 100, 118

"I Have Known Rivers" (Hughes), 118
"In the Morning" (Dunbar), 98, 118, 125
Individual contact, 32
Initial teaching alphabet, 31-32

Jobs, relating education to, 79-80, 138
Johnson, James Weldon, 83, 99, 118
Johnson, Lyndon B., 110, 112

Klausmeier, Herbert, 144
Kornberg, Leonard, 27-28

Language, overcoming distortions in, 84-86
Let Us Break Bread Together, 111

Listen, overcoming inability to, 82-84, 125-126
Louis, Joe, 80
Lying, 36

"Ma Lord" (Hughes), 98
Mary Jane (Sterling), 81, 94
Mathematical materials, 123
Mays, Willie, 98
Miel, Alice, 10
Misbehavior, typical forms of, 32-40
Mobility of ghetto population, 34, 132
Money management, teaching of, 74-75, 78-79
Morland, Kenneth, 79
Myrdal, Gunnar, 23

Narcotics addiction, 137
    children's awareness of, 69, 77, 95
Natchez, Gladys, 87
Negro Family in the United States (Frazier), 25
Negro history and culture, teaching of, 97-101
New student, problems of, 34
New teacher:
    case example of, 48-58
    tasks for, 142, 144-146
New York City school boycott, 103-104, 135
Nutrition, teaching of, 74-75

Ojemann, Ralph, 40
Organization, classroom, 28-30, 46-47, 82
    See also Routine; Structure.
Ottley, Roi, 23
Out-of-school activities, teacher participation in, 43-44

Patterson, Floyd, 98
Personalization of subject matter, 45-46
Pictures, flat, classroom use of, 120-122
Playground, problems of, 34

Index

Police, overcoming hostility to, 108-109
Profanity, 24, 32, 37-38
Projectors, opaque and overhead, 122
P.S. 79 school district, New York City, 9, 127-140
    automobile accidents in, 129-130
    business establishments in, 136
    families on welfare in, 133
    housing in, 127-131
    median educational attainment in, 134
    mobility of population in, 132
    occupations of inhabitants of, 133-134
    parental attitudes toward school in, 139-140
    religious influence in, 134-135
    unemployment in, 132-133, 138
P.S. 103, New York City, 9, 128

Reading Disability (Roswell and Natchez), 87
Reading problems, 86-88
Records, phonograph, 124
Redl, Fritz, 25
Restlessness, 38-39
Rewards, use of, 27-28
Rexograph materials, 116-118
Riessman, Frank, 62
Robeson, Paul, 112
Roswell, Florence, 87
Routine, classroom, 47
    See also Organization; Structure.
Rustin, Bayard, 113

Sands, Diana, 112
Smalls, Robert, 99
Stealing, 36-37
Sterling, Dorothy, 81, 94
Structure:
    definition of, 26
    need for, 25-27

174

Successful teaching:
   attitudes that lead to, 41-47
   case example of, 48-58
   children's views of, 59-64, 66-67
   See also Curriculum.

Tattling, 35-36
Taylor, Marvin, 9
Teacher (Ashton-Warner), 18, 86
Teaching in the Elementary School (Klausmeier, *et al.*), 144
Teletrainer, 122
Television, use of, in schools, 120
Thoreau, Henry, 42
Thumb-sucking, among ghetto schoolchildren, 68
To Sir, with Love (Braithwaite), 18
Truancy, 39-40
Trubowitz, Naomi, 10
Tubman, Harriet, 99
Turner, Charles, 99

Washington, Booker T., 100-101
Welfare, Dept. of:
   dependence on and attitudes toward, 133
   teaching about operations of, 105-107
What Secondary Schools Can Do About Teenage Narcotics Addiction, 77
Wheatley, Phillis, 99
Wilkins, Roy, 113
Wilkinson, Frances, 40
Wineman, David, 25
Winters, Shelley, 112
Wittich, Walter, 144
Workbooks, 119
Wright, Benjamin, 32

Yashima, Taro, 94
Youth in the Ghetto (HARYOU report), 97, 143